CONTENTS

Introduction

SECTION ONE

SECTION THREE:

Chapter 1: Tools and Tips   164

Introduction

When discussing customer service, a FTSE 100 MD said in 2005;
"That's very interesting, but it all sounds like blindingly obvious common sense to me."
Three years later the value of the organisation was less than 1/10th of its value at the time of that statement.

In today's fast moving world, businesses and economies are changing at an astonishing pace, with the result that systems and technologies that were cutting edge yesterday are obsolete today.

No matter what your business, whether an international conglomerate, national institution, small business, not-for-profit organisation, or a one man band, the only way you will stay ahead of change and build a long-term profitable future is by:

- Firstly, delivering top quality services to customers consistently and excellently and
- Secondly, continually listening to them effectively in order to understand their true and future needs.

Why this work was written

'Great or Poor' is an idea born out of frustration.

I have been to lots of presentations and talks on customer service and they always seem to be saying the same thing:

"It's important to give great customer service."

To me, this seems to be BOCS

'Blindingly Obvious Common Sense'

So the REAL question which no one seems to be asking, or more importantly, answering is:

**'If it's blindingly obvious common sense,
why isn't it blissfully normal common practice?'**

This book seeks to find some real answers to this VITAL question and three crucial other ones.

1. If customers are 'satisfied' with a service, why do they defect to another one?
2. What can we do about it?
3. And how do we measure it?

This book aims to present the answers to the above conundrum in a short, simple and easy to implement style. This is NOT a bible of 'customer service tools and ideas', this is a book you can understand in a couple of days, teach your colleagues and recommend to your friends.

Ultimately, the aim of this book is to make a **huge difference to you and your organisation** and to help you **actually deliver great service each and every day**, in all that you do.

Thanks for buying it. I hope it achieves this for you.

Best Wishes

Guy Arnold

(And please refer to the end of this book, for your Special Introductory Offer of 20% off your first Consultancy or Training with us).

Credit and Thanks

I'd like to thank all my colleagues and customers, past and present, who have helped to clarify this material.

Chris Edwards for his help and amusing stories.

Guy Insull and Natalie Dee from the Champions Club for their support and encouragement.

Mary Cummings for doing all the legwork so excellently and considerately, with a new baby in the house!

Stephen Covey and Rob Parsons for their support and inspiration, without which this work could not have been written.

Linda Arnold for teaching me to be very fussy with service from an early age!

Simon Arnold for his support and love.

My children for constantly testing my will and ability to actually do some of this.

And last, but by no means least, my wife Alison, for pointing out that this was all blindingly obvious common sense in the first place and for spending endless hours reading through draft copies and believing in me.

SECTION ONE

Chapter One: What's the Problem?

"Even my mother in law likes this place!" Customer feedback from a busy pub in the UK

It seems we've all 'got along fine' for the past 4000 years, without having to worry too much about customer service - so why rock the boat now?

Here's an alternative view of the past.

We started off as hunter/gatherers:

In this society there were pretty clear roles of the sexes and little need for 'customer service' outside of the tribe or group.

About 4000 years ago, things began to change:

The world went through the Agrarian Revolution (not commonly covered in Western history books). People started getting organised and output increased tenfold. This had a number of impacts on the world.

People had to 'specialise':

- People had to start getting on with strangers
- Production and production capability exploded
- This opened the way to 'civilisation' as we know it

From a 'customer service' point of view, the real issue was that for the first time, people had to start trusting relative strangers to provide service and systematically deal with people outside their immediate group.

The idea of customer service was born (though call centres were still a long way off!).

About 300 years ago, things changed again:

The much fabled Industrial Revolution started. People stopped living and dealing with people 'they knew' and moved to large cities to get work and feed the kids. This is covered widely in modern history books, but they often fail to mention the real issue here.

Factually, what happened was:

1. A global shift of power from Agrarian to industrial economies.
2. Mass migration to towns and cities (still happening all over the world - this revolution isn't yet complete).
3. Breakdown of traditional laws and values (including the rise of institutional laws and values).
4. Splitting up of extended families, in effect, a completely dysfunctional transformation from the way we have been genetically programmed to live, work and play.
5. The consequent issues this has caused for society are painfully clear all around us.

What's the problem?

From a 'customer service' point of view, this had enormous repercussions.

Initially there was little need for good service, as everything was new and hard to come by. Most people were basically struggling to survive (when you send a seven-year old boy up a chimney, there's little point in telling the chimney owner to "have a nice day now", or offering a guarantee on soot removal or refund if the child got stuck up there).

As time moved on, however, things began to change and as the new became commonplace, the commonplace needed a differentiating factor, i.e. 'customer service'. With rates of change and innovation continuing to accelerate, we see this happening in ever decreasing time frames today.

But there was a problem. The **'industrial age mindset'** was the problem, and it manifested itself like this.

Everyone needs to eat - so factory owners could 'get away with murder' (as indeed some organisations do to this day). They found that the most effective way to get people to do what they wanted them to do was the 'carrot and stick' method. This worked well, when people were struggling to survive. You paid for and got, their bodily work … but their minds… well, who cared?

But what happened when times changed? The new became commonplace and the overriding need was for innovation, flexibility and service. Yes, you've guessed it. Does the word 'British Leyland' come to mind? The 'workers' weren't interested. They'd been treated badly, so they responded badly and promptly put their organisations out of business (and themselves out of jobs) through restrictive practices, unreliability and profoundly poor service (in all areas).

How did (and do) the managers react? Simple, they:

- Got bigger sticks and carrots
- Did some 'motivational training'
- Started studying 'customer service', made departments just for this, and told people what to do and how to do it

Did this work? Well, yes, a bit. Until something better came along, it made a bit of difference, but as Einstein said:

"The problems we face cannot be resolved at the same level of thinking we were at when we created them."

So it was only a 'sticking plaster'. And the plaster soon fell off when the next revolution came along. (More on this to follow). But, unfortunately, many organisations have yet to realise this!

And this is why businesses are growing and dying at such a breathtaking pace today. They find a 'gap in the market', they fill it, but they don't get their internal customers (i.e. their own employees) properly motivated, so in turn, they can't give great service to their external customer. Someone else comes along who can do this, uses their idea and then takes their business. It happens all the time.

But before we talk about the next revolution, let's just examine what we've learnt from the above alternative history lesson.

The points to learn are:

- Each revolution produces a massive increase in production and production capability: so people can do and have more.

- Revolutions change everything: skills that worked well in the last revolution now become restrictive and can put you out of business overnight - and everyone loves change, don't they?

- Revolutions are coming at us with ever decreasing time between them: so the need for change is pressing and continuous – a major issue for hunter gatherers who are not genetically built to thrive on change.

Remember Darwin's law: *'In order to survive, you have to adapt'* (and at a rate that's literally breathtaking in the world today).

The geographic regions that led in the previous revolution will always lag in the next one. The Middle East led the Agrarian Revolution and has been struggling to compete in the industrial age. The West led the Industrial Revolution and now we're in the middle of another revolution. World power is shifting (see below) to the East.

About 30 years ago, things started to change yet again!

Posterity will be the judge, but it seems that we're now in the middle of yet another more powerful Revolution: the 'Knowledge Revolution'. A significant proportion of the world's population now don't have to worry about a roof over their head or food in their mouths, and they have:

- An overwhelming availability of 'time saving' gadgets (an interesting topic in itself and the subject of a future book)
- Unlimited information, available free of charge via the Internet
- A truly global economy
- The opening of borders across the globe
- Over-supply of goods and services
- Business transparency (combined with a severe lack of trust)
- Major environmental issues

This has a HUGE impact on the way we live, work and play. From a customer service perspective, it means that:

- The customer has almost unlimited choice
- The customer can easily search out the best deals
- There is mass migration of workers across international boundaries (keen to do the job twice as well for half the pay of existing workers)
- The customer can easily give instant feedback for millions of others to see
- The smallest lapse of trust and service can become an organisation's killer overnight
- In effect, customer service becomes the single most important factor in business success today (and for the foreseeable future). Worse still, what is 'great' today, will be commonplace tomorrow.

It also means that the carrot and stick 'industrial age' mindset doesn't really work any more. And this doesn't just apply to Companies. It applies to Governments and Countries in just the same way.

Here's an example of what can happen if you don't get this right:

Netscape:

10 years ago they had about 90% of the Internet browser market. Yet, at the time of writing, their share is 0.6% in a hugely expanding market!!

And here's an example of what happens when you do get this right.

Enterprise Rent a Car

Enterprise Rent a Car may not seem to be the most exciting business you've ever heard of, but it has a fascinating story to tell: from a tiny, one shop operation in the basement of a car dealership 50 years ago, it has evolved into one of the greatest modern-day examples of how to build a phenomenally successful company through delivering outstanding customer service at all times.

It's size is impressive:

- $9bn turnover
- 7000 locations around the world
- The biggest car buyer in the world
- Highest credit rating in it's industry
- In the Forbes top 20 Companies in America
- Has never laid off employees

But what really makes the difference is that it has achieved this amazing prosperity in a highly competitive market, whilst being surrounded by other businesses closing, merging and generally struggling with low morale and dissatisfied customers.

How has Enterprise done it? Above all, it adheres to the 'blindingly obvious common sense' philosophy set forth by company founder Jack Taylor back on day one: "Take care of your customers and employees, and the profits will follow."

This is taken to mean that having "satisfied" customers isn't enough: they look to create passionate devotees. We'll demonstrate later how the figures back this up, but as customers of other businesses we know it's true.

The strategy is clearly effective: it is excellently regarded by all rating agencies, it is consistently rated as one of the best Companies to work for in America, it achieves profitability way above average whilst delivering great service and true value for money, and it's business model is virtually recession proof!

What more could you want?

(For more details on Enterprise Rent a Car, please see www.exceedingcustomerexpectations.com)

Here's my Vision:

We are in the middle of a Knowledge Revolution, significantly greater in impact than the Industrial Revolution. The Internet and explosion of information it has generated, will empower the customer unlike anything that has gone before. It has also created a truly global economy.

On top of this, the customer (previously disempowered and abused by misleading adverts and clever marketing) will become ever more demanding and unforgiving.

'Satisfied' customers are no longer good enough. Cutting edge service is winning business globally at an astonishing pace and 'traditional' businesses are becoming extinct almost overnight.

In order to prosper in the future, an organisation's service must be 'great', because if not, it will be 'poor'.

For companies to thrive (or even survive) in this brave new world, they MUST anticipate, listen and react to their customers' views and needs. They will need to have an exceptional level of service to begin with, and then listen to customers' additional needs on top of this. If they only react to what customers say, they may always be one step behind.

Existing systems and mindsets make this very hard for organisations to deal with. This book will explore (and find simple answers to) these issues and here's some thinking to get us going.

Let's start with some hotel feedback from the Internet. (I knew exactly where to go, this hotel chain is the best in the world).

"First time at this hotel and I was so impressed with the flowers, the staff and the location. Will certainly go back the next time I am in New York. Have been telling all my family and friends that they must go there. Awesome."

"Customer service was excellent. Hotel radiated class and elegance."

"The 'xxxx' exceeds any hotel I have ever visited. Customer support was outstanding. Room service was quick and friendly. The hotel is simply beautiful."

"Everything about the 'xxxx'was more than I expected. It will be my hotel of choice for every New York visit."

"Helpful and polite staff. ***Seem to have a system."***

These are standard reviews for a leading hotel in New York. Read any reviews on this hotel and you'll see the same thing. Yes, it's expensive, it can afford to be. It's consistently excellent!

This hotel knows a secret and this is the secret that I am going to impart to you in this book. As with all secrets, it's blindingly obvious common sense and this secret is:

You can take a horse to water, but you can't make it drink!

How many times have we heard:

"I told them to do this, and they still haven't done it. I can't understand why they're so lazy / uncooperative / etc"?
… the horse isn't thirsty!

Now the hotel chain above obviously knows something about this. Their Mission is 100% customer delight and they make this work with communication, procedures, incentives, awards and involvement. Now the horse knows what it needs to do to drink and starts feeling thirsty because it knows that it has to drink in order to survive and grow in this organisation - a breakthrough!

Compare this to the statement given in 2008, to Maasai warriors running in the London Marathon.

'Many people do not smile in the UK, as they work in jobs they do not enjoy'.

So there are two chances of receiving great customer service from these people:

'Fat' and 'slim'

There's a pub in Somerset, England that has increased turnover by 1000% in under a year under new management and they embody the crux of the solution. This is what they do:

They have a clear VISION, centred on the gap in the market and how they can fulfil a vital social need by filling it well.

They have a clear MISSION based on how the customer will feel, if they fulfil the VISION well. It is 'for every customer to leave with a smile on their face, keen to come again'. Good, simple stuff (and not a mention of being the best, generating shareholder returns or bottom line profits!)

They have values that align behaviour to achieving the MISSION and all their strategies and processes spring from it: for example

- They don't maximise gross profit - they give the best they can at the most competitive price possible: And they're very busy.

- All staff can work towards achieving the Mission, from the Chef making excellent, delicious food, to the cleaners ensuring that the pub/loos are always clean - all of which contributes to the customers leaving with a smile on their face.

- Staff don't have official titles, their job description is simple: they are there 'to enable every customer to leave with a smile on their face, keen to come again'. And they're very empowered.

- They don't advertise (because they believe that, if you're good enough, advertising should be unnecessary), it's all by word of mouth: Yet they turn away hundreds of people every week.

- They measure their 'great or poor' score on a monthly basis and publish this to all the staff, alongside the P&L: And they act on scores by:

  - Thanking them when it's good
  - Identifying and acting on any issues raised
  - Incentivising high scores
  - And, not surprisingly, the level of tips reflects the score
  - So staff continue to be happy and motivated

So what does this tell us? Simply, that there is a way to deliver excellent service consistently and it's this (following the horse and water analogy!):

1. The water needs to be available
2. The horse needs to know how, where and why to drink
3. The horse needs to want to drink
4. and probably, the horse needs consistent encouragement

So why is this so hard to achieve?

*   Without huge effort
*   During periods of immense change
*   On an ongoing basis

And how do we know we're achieving it?

This is the conundrum facing all businesses today and the answer will be found in the following pages.

For now there's some *bad* news and some *good* news.

> *The bad news:* Telling the horse to drink or we'll beat it doesn't work. (This is the Industrial Age mindset).
> *The good news:* Horses are generally thirsty, indeed they have to drink to survive (and this can work for or against you).

There are some common issues that prevent horses from drinking:

*   They don't know where the water is
*   They don't like the taste of the water
*   They don't like the water-keeper
*   They're thirsty but can't get to the water
*   Other thirstier horses have pushed them out of the way
*   They don't know they're thirsty

These are the problems we'll resolve.

"There is no higher religion than human service. To work for the common good is the greatest creed." Albert Schweitzer

Chapter Two: Why are we here?

"For myself I am an optimist: it doesn't seem to be much use being anything else." Winston Churchill.
"What do we live for if it is not to make life less difficult for each other?" George Eliot

It seems appropriate at this early stage to answer this question which has been perplexing mankind since time began. And my answer is: **God knows**! But, it makes no sense to do things averagely, when can you do things excellently. In other words, most of us have no idea of the meaning of life (and wars are constantly fought over it), but putting this aside, it makes sense to do things as well as you can because:

- It's much more fulfilling.
- It opens up opportunities.
- It stops waste.
- The more you put in, the more you get out.
- It's a pretty good bet that, whatever the purpose of life, we'll probably be doing something right when we do our best!
- It's the only way to achieve immortality.

So, back to reality. A question I start with in my training programmes is:

Why are we in business?

This applies to traditional 'profit making' and 'not for profit' organisations alike and the answer I always get first is:

"To make money!"

The response to this always is:

Then you must either: Double your prices and halve your costs or work for the Mint

At this stage, delegates start to look at me in a funny way and eye the exits in case of escape.   But the point is this: the only way to make profits is to give the right product or service, at the right price, in the right way.   Or, in other words:

We are in business to deliver a service that is so good that people are prepared to pay a fair price for it

So, we're in business to give a service, not to make money. The marvellous thing is that this is a simple equation:

The better the service you give: the more money you will make

Another startling example of 'Blindingly Obvious Common Sense' or BOCS as we shall call it.

Let's look at what's happening in the world today. With new and innovative products and services, having high selling prices and producing great profits (e.g. Apple do this well).

But, very quickly (and increasingly so), the 'new' becomes the 'norm' and all your competitors catch up. 300 years ago, it would take years or decades for competitors to catch up. Today it takes months, or even weeks.

Thus, the only way to make good profits for the long term is to 'begin with the end in mind' (with thanks to Stephen Covey: 'The 7 Habits of Highly Effective People'. I advise you to buy it and read it, it's one of the best self-improvement books ever written). Give the best service at the best price from the start. If you're good enough, you'll thrive, if not, at least you'll know before you've invested your life savings!

The next question I then ask at my training sessions is:

"What is 'profit'?"

This floors the delegates - even the accountants can only be heard mumbling about 'net' and 'gross' at the back of the room... something only they barely understand. But the reality is this:

Profit is the 'premium' you can charge for the service you deliver!

Now we know what we're talking about.

But often, people reply with the following phrases:

- "It's tough out there"
- "In reality it's not like that"
- "Price is more important than service"

To which I reply (in order):

1. "Yes, that's why it's so important to get your service right: the worse you do this, the tougher it will be for you."

2. "Reality is what you make it":

   a. If your attitude is 'I'll believe it when I see it' (the great 'glass half empty' view), then you'll be right
   b. If your attitude is 'I'll see it when I believe it' (the great 'glass half full' view) then you'll be right.
   c. Give it a go. If it's so awful 'out there' then surely things can't get any worse.
   d. I love the quote from Henry Ford and have it stuck on my office wall:
   "If you think you can, or you think you can't, you're probably right".

3. "Yes, price is important, you always have to charge a fair price for the long term, but it's ONLY more important than service when there are no other discerning factors".

   If your customer trades with you purely because of the price, what they are really telling you is that your service could do with some improvement!

Some more views on price, before we move on:

- If price is your 'unique selling proposition', then in reality, you haven't got a unique selling proposition.

- If you win business on price, then you'll lose it on price. The ONLY long term factor for success is great customer service, producing customer loyalty.

- There was a fantastic example of this in the UK in 2008, when a 'Poundland' shop was put out of business by a '99p shop' next door!

Be transparent on price: if you're more expensive, be open and tell your customers why. They'll often opt for the more expensive but more transparent option (because it engenders trust). Some examples of this:

- Amazon.com: tell you all the different price options on products they sell or source.

- Waitrose supermarkets in the UK: promote quality and service over price, and enjoy consistent growth and good profits.

- Stella Artois was always promoted as 'reassuringly expensive' in the UK during the 1990s, where it was the No. 1 premium lager by a huge margin. (Incidentally, this was fatally undermined when supermarkets started doing discount price deals on it and promptly removed the unique selling point!)

- A curious, but real, economic fact: the more you pay for something, then the more it's worth (disposable income has been growing across the World ever since the Second World War. Charge a fair price for a great service!)

- There are only two crimes in business:

  Doing business below your profit threshold

  Not doing business above it

  From the economic turmoil in 2008 and 2009, it seems that many very highly paid business people don't yet understand this!

And when we're the customer, we all know that when it comes to cost, we ask ourselves:

"Would I consider booking a week's holiday in a villa by the beach for £99 per person including flights, or is it too good to be true?"

Cost reflects the offering, if the same holiday was advertised at £495 per person you would explore further. I can imagine the holiday for £99. Yes, and so can you!

Here are some other examples:

A whisky company some 30 years ago launched an expensive blended whisky. They advertised the fact that if you did not earn more than £20,000 a year, then you could not afford it. Sales went through the roof. People wanted to be seen as high flyers, so perceived the whisky to be as excellent as it was expensive.

Why are we here?

There is a fish and chip shop in the UK called Hanbury's. There are two other fish and chip shops within 100 yards. Hanbury's sells its fish and chips at almost three times the price of the other two, yet it is by far the busiest. Why? Because the service, quality and experience are much, much better.

(Remember, to the customer, the quality of your product is as much a part of your service to them as the way in which it is delivered).

As noted, with further thanks, to Stephen Covey's 'The 7 Habits of Highly Effective People', the ONLY long term effective way to do business is to:

- **Begin with the end in mind.**
- **Go for a 'win/win' outcome. This is called 'good profit':** This point is worthy of a book in itself, but suffice to say, win/win is the ONLY long-term effective business solution because the only other options are:
  a. **Win/lose: This is called 'bad profit':** You win the sale, but you upset your customer (not very sensible, but very often what innovators or monopolies do and then wonder why they go out of business when competitors come along).

  b. **Lose/win: This is called 'no profit':** You get loads of business, but you make a loss (the paths of the history of commerce are littered with victims here, you could open a restaurant with 'all you can eat for £5' and put on The Rolling Stones - you'd be busy, but not very successful).

  c. **Lose/lose:** Self-explanatory.

  d. **The other alternative to win/win, and the only viable alternative, is called 'No Deal':** This is where you don't do business, but you keep talking and cooperating - this can be very powerful in the long-term, but may need patience.

Why can Starbucks charge 3 or 4 times as much as others close by for a cup of coffee, if price is so important?

Here are some great reasons NOT to deal with people on price only:

- They take up all your time
- They complain the most
- They pay late, if at all
- They upset other customers
- They're disloyal
- They destroy the credibility of your full priced goods and services
- They steal ideas and information

I think that's enough on price then!

Now that we know why we are in business and what profit is, we will need to ask ourselves:

Who in my business/department/team know this?

How does my/our activities relate to this?

Many people won't know this and if that's the case, how on earth can they help me/us/our organisation deliver that fantastic service and thereby make the money that we want? The horse is confused at best and unable to drink at worst. When this happens, it comes to work thirsty and eventually 'dead'. So service plummets. That's one reason why BOCS often isn't Blissfully Normal Common Practice ('BNCP')!

Please take time to do the following exercise.

Exercise: Discovering Your Vision and Making Money

	Your Organisation	You/Your Department
What's the 'Vision' (i.e. why are we here?)		
What's the 'service' we give that makes the money?		
Is this a 'worthwhile' service?		
Does all my team/ department / organisation know this?		
Is it clear how our activities relate to the service that makes the money?		
In an ideal world what would the best service in the world in our market look like? (This may generate great ideas for improvement and development)		

You can see that I've included a column for 'your organisation' and 'you/your department'.

The point is that if your own Vision and values are aligned to those of your organisation, then great, you can help them drive forward towards 'success'.

If not, then you need to be asking yourself why you're spending your valuable time doing all of this every day and what else might you be doing instead?

There are four victims when someone is in the wrong occupation:

- The organisation: because you'll never be able to deliver great service if you're unfulfilled and often you'll actually be a drain on them.

- You: no one on their deathbed has said: 'I'm glad I slaved away in the job I hated for 40 years so that I could get that index linked pension'.

- The poor customer: who has to listen to your moans (and suffer 'Fawlty Towers' levels of service).

- Everyone.

Has this raised some issues? Do you need to speak to others in your organisation?

Probably? Good, you're normal.

List here any actions within your influence, that you need to take to clarify or change anything that has come up from the above exercise.

-
-
-
-
-
-
-
-
-

List here issues that you can't influence, but that need clarifying or changing.

Issues	Who I need to speak to
-	
-	
-	
-	
-	
-	
-	

Also make an appointment in your diary/planner to action this at work today (or at least tomorrow ... I'll give you tonight to think it over!). And, of course, we're always available to help. Please see our contact details at the end of this book.

Remember:

'No farmer ever ploughed his field by turning it over in his mind'.

TAKE SOME ACTION WITHIN THE NEXT 24 HOURS, OR YOU NEVER WILL.

Now, back to the point.

The fact that we're all here to deliver a service that is so good that people are prepared to pay a premium for it, is a very simple, obvious, common sense statement. It's also a very simple strategy for business success.

But it's very hard to make it work in practice. We'll find out why and what to do about this in the next chapter, but here's an outline of what's needed in order to achieve this.

What's needed to deliver great customer service?

Over and over again, companies and organisations announce 'reorganisations', 'refocuses' and 'new initiatives' based around delivering great customer service. These are generally well intentioned, but more often or not they fail. It sounds simple and easy (and BOCS) but it's hugely hard to make it work in reality. Success can only be delivered by:

- EVERYONE (yes, everyone, not just the customer facing staff. A chain is only as strong as its weakest link) being focused OBSESSIVELY on the needs of the customer.
- Irrespective of their roles and duties.
- Irrespective of 'company procedure', 'year end deadlines', 'profit margins', 'budgets' and all the other lame and irritating excuses that drive the customer wild.

This requires a huge leap of faith, from the top to the bottom and from the bottom to the top, in any organisation, namely:

"If we do this we will achieve success", not "We'll only do it if....

- budgets aren't tight"
- profits aren't affected"
- policy isn't bent"

Because if you deviate from the overriding aim to deliver great service in any way at any time, this not only alienates the customer, more importantly it sends a HUGE signal to your staff. What you're effectively saying is 'we're not really serious about this' or 'you can only deliver great service when we decide you can', resulting in your staff reacting, 'if I don't know when or if I can, it's best to play it safe and not bother'.

So success can only be delivered by management teams who understand this great conundrum.

1. They must be personally obsessive about delivering great customer service. This is absolutely crucial and unfortunately somewhat rare. We see around us organisations that are led by people who take this very seriously (See 'Good to Great' by Jim Collins - well worth reading). Unfortunately, we also see the ruins of organisations that have been led by people with other motivations.

2. Have no hidden agenda. This IS the agenda and no other. Otherwise it can't work.

3. Understand the magnitude of the task. It's much more than saying 'have a nice day'!

4. Be brave enough to really put a Customer Focused Mission at the heart of their organisation/team/department (more on this later).

Focusing efforts on driving this difficult task forward may seem easy. However, if you imagine that there are only two human motivations, namely:

'Away from': which means away from sources of discomfort or pain and
'Towards': which means towards sources of pleasurable profit

Then it is, in fact, the manager or the leader's task to make delivering a poor service painful, unattractive and personally unprofitable, while at the same time making delivering a great service fun, exciting and rewarding in all circumstances. This is not easy, but this book will show you how to do this simply and effectively.

Let's look at an example of an organisation that does this really well:

Pike Place Fish Market in Seattle:

Some of you will have been lucky enough to have seen the Pike Place Fish Market training video called 'FISH!', or even better to have visited the market itself in Seattle. If you haven't done either of these, don't worry, the video is available and there are many books on it.

What they do really well is this: They have agreed between them that their Vision is to 'be world famous' and they have also agreed four key values that help them achieve this task.

These values are:

- **Play:** i.e. Have fun at work!

- **Be there:** i.e. Be the best that you can, at the job that you're doing, while you're doing it and focus only on the job in hand, to avoid being distracted and not giving the best service possible. (They have fun when they try and explain this particular value to bankers and accountants and other professionals, as it sounds so silly!).

- **Make their day:** this one is self explanatory and surely should be a value of every person in every service industry!

- **Choose your attitude:** this means that it makes no sense to be miserable at anything you do because, whether you like to admit it or not, you are choosing to do it.

In my training sessions, we do a fun exercise called the 'have to' list. I start by asking people to compile a list of all the things they 'HAVE TO' do when they get home. I then ask a brave soul to share two or three things from their list. When they do this, I ask them on each point 'what would happen if you didn't do it?'

So let's do this exercise now:

Exercise: 10 things you 'have to' do later today

1	
2	
3	
4	
5	
6	
7	
8	
9	
10	

Now, stop and ask yourself:

"What would happen it I didn't do it?"

Make a list of your answers here:

1	
2	
3	
4	
5	
6	
7	
8	
9	
10	

The point here is that we CHOOSE to do everything we do (except die and take up space). Think about it for a while. Every action or omission that we choose to do has a natural consequence. We have no power over the consequence, but complete power over what we choose to do.

For example, if I own a cat, one of my jobs at the end of the day will be to feed it. If I feed it, it will live and probably quite like me. If I don't, it will go hungry and either die or go hunting.

So, whether I feed it or not, has a consequence and when asked that question above, I might say 'I have to feed the cat this evening'. The point is, I don't actually 'have to' feed the cat, I 'choose' to because I want the consequences of doing it.

Seems logical - what's the real point?

The real point is that we choose to do everything in our lives. In fact our choices have got us to where we are now (sorry to mention this, I find this hard too - just ask my wife and kids!).

Now redo the above exercise, replacing 'have to' with 'choose to', 'want to', 'am going to' and then write in 'why'.

E.g. I choose to go to work	Because I like what I do and want to have a good quality of life.
	Because
	Because
	Because
	Because
	Because
	Because
	Because
	Because
	Because

So none of us 'has to' go to work!

We 'choose' to go to work because we want the consequences of doing it, for example:

- Money
- Being busy
- Being with people
- Forming relationships
- Doing something worthwhile
- Working as a team
- Etc

This may seem like a pointless point, but, until we accept this, we cannot move forward and accept that we have the power to change everything in our lives, for example, in the way we deal with people and of course in the way we approach customer service in our roles.

The language we use gives away our feelings, and in this case we must change 'have to' to 'want to' or 'choose to' or 'am going to'. And, if we cannot do this, (i.e. we cannot bear ourselves saying these words differently), we must then ask ourselves why we are doing what we do.

Because if we don't want to or choose to be doing this, we can never be 'great' at it and give 'great' customer service. There are no exceptions. If we 'want to' go to work, we are much more likely to be able to 'choose our attitude' and thus deliver excellent service and by the way, achieve success, however that is measured in our role.

Back to Pike Place Fish!

Whilst there is some conflict as to whether the official 'Fish!' merchandise (which is quite expensive, but very good), really represents the true situation at the fish market is up for debate, but it's clearly a fantastically fun and profitable organisation and I urge you to check them out. Do all, or as many as possible, of the things on this list, as you'll pick up invaluable tips for your own business.

- Look at their Website: www.pikeplacefish.com
- Read their book : available on their website
- Read the other FISH! Books: available from all good booksellers
- See the videos: www.videotraining.com

In a nutshell, the point of this chapter is this:

- It's hard to deliver a great customer service and standard consistently and excellently - very hard!

- The organisation has to have a Mission and Vision, within which customer service excellence is the hub that drives everything else.

- This will naturally enable great customer service within all other systems processes and behaviour.

The people at Pike Place Fish have achieved fun, fame and of course profitability, only because they have a Vision and Mission that places

World famous customer service at its core

This is 'secret No. 1', and we call it having a:

CUSTOMER FOCUSED MISSION

You will see consistent referral to Customer Focused Mission throughout this book, and for ease of reference I will refer to it as CFM from now on.

Having a CFM is an absolutely crucial point and all too often, while I am consulting with people, it becomes very clear (as it's usually the first question I ask) that:

- Their organisation, department, or section has no clear Vision at all of what the business opportunity for the future is, or what success in the future looks like for them.

- There is no clear, simple, Customer Focused Mission statement for the whole organisation.

- In fact, to borrow the words of Stephen Covey again, ' They are so busy sawing down the tree, that they don't have time to sharpen the saw.'

Without a clear, unambiguous and obsessively Customer Focused Mission, the roots of any organisation are shallow and when the storm comes, all sorts of damage will occur.

The Mission (more in the next chapter) is the root of all activity and behaviour. Get this wrong and there's little chance of delivering the excellent customer service you seek.

Before we finish this chapter, I would like to mention one more thing:

Habits

Some quotes:

"First we make our habits, then our habits make us." Stephen Covey
"We are what we repeatedly do. Excellence then, is not an act, but a habit." Aristotle

Habits are very important when we are talking about excellent customer service, because habits guide us particularly, when the going gets tough. Habits are curious things and come from a number of sources:

- Experience
- Environment
- Upbringing
- Genetics

But, (contrary to what my parents say), we do have the power to change our habits! When the going is easy (the sun is out and you have a hot date lined up for the evening) giving excellent customer service in any circumstance is a doddle. However, it's when circumstances toughen up, that the real test arises of how great you are at giving service.

As individuals and as organisations, we need to develop habits to drive great Customer Focused behaviour in all circumstances - particularly the tough ones. A CFM is the basis by which to achieve this (both personally and organisationally), backed up with training, feedback, encouragement and motivation.

More on all the above later, but for now I would just like you to take a moment to list your habits, good and bad and then shut the book and spend some time thinking about how these habits affect your ability to deliver customer service consistently and excellently, both personally and organisationally.

[For further detailed thought and action points on habits, please read 'The 7 Habits of Highly Effective People']

Exercise: Habits
Personally:

We are often very good at self criticism for bad habits (except for a boss I once worked for), but we rarely take the time to consider the good ones and how they benefit us and those around us. Make a point of also taking some time over your good habits and encourage yourself to repeat them as often as possible. The more you encourage people (you and others around you), the better you'll get - this is very important.

Good Habits	Effect on 'customer service' (and your own ability to perform and succeed in your role).

Bad Habits	Effect on 'customer service' (and your own ability to perform and succeed in your role).

Organisationally:

Good Habits	Effect on 'customer service' (and your own ability to perform and succeed in your role).

Bad Habits	Effect on 'customer service' (and your own ability to perform and succeed in your role).

What actions do I need to take to start addressing these?

Personal Actions:
-
-
-
-
-
-
-
-
-

Organisational actions (if you can't influence the actual issue, what can you do or who can you speak to at least do something) . *"Action is the antidote to despair."* Joan Baez

Organisational Actions:
-
-
-
-
-
-
-

Here's a great story to round off this Chapter and lead us into the next one, where we will be talking about the principles of great customer service and the financial costs and opportunities involved.

There was once a salesman called Tom, who enjoyed his job. He had a great personality and sold his product well, largely it has to be said, due to his personality skills and a caring attitude.

Then along came the new Sales Director who spent time looking at the call sheets. He said that the sales force was not making enough calls in a day and he wanted to see a call rate of 12 customers a day.

At the next sales meeting, the Director asked Tom why, on one day, he only did 10 calls. The reply came back, "Sorry, someone stopped me to ask me what I was selling."

And here's a story that aroused my attention from the Press (from 'The Week' in September 2008 which illustrates the point that we are often so tied up in 'doing our job' that we forget the real, underlying purpose of that job).

It was a bad week for the Police (in the UK), who were accused of being unresponsive and rude to the public.

"Over half of the complaints against the Police are about rudeness, incivility and lack of service," admitted Ian Johnston, President of the Police Superintendents' Association. "We need to pay attention to that."

Conclusion:

Very little of this is new thinking. Here are some ancient quotes on this subject.

"He who secures the good of others has already secured his own." Confucius

"Love thy neighbour." Jesus

"All that we are is the result of what we have thought. If a man speaks or acts with an evil thought, pain follows him. If a man speaks or acts with a pure thought, happiness follows him, like a shadow that never leaves him." Gandhi

But in the hard, 'dog eat dog' world of international commerce, the message seems to have got lost a bit!

And here's a great quote to finish the Chapter with.

"Your work is to discover your work and then with all your heart to give yourself to it." Buddha

Chapter Three : What Matters?

"A golden key can open any door." Ancient Proverb.

The 7 Deadly Sins', according to Mahatma Gandhi:

Wealth without work
 Pleasure without conscience
 Knowledge without character
 Commerce without morality (business without ethics)
 Science without humanity
 Religion without sacrifice
 Politics without principle

I wonder if the 2008/9 economic crisis has some roots in the violation of these principles perchance?

A personal story:

In the early 1990's, when my wife and I were newly married, we decided to throw in two good well paid jobs, and buy a dilapidated and bankrupt country pub in Devon, England. Why did we do this? There were three principal reasons:

1. The property market had crashed and it was a great opportunity.
2. I was involved in the pub business, taking on bankrupt businesses and turning them around, so I thought it would be a good idea to do it for myself.
3. It seemed like a good idea at the time, and we were young enough to go bankrupt and bounce back if necessary.

Everything went well for a while, and business started booming.

Then winter arrived, and interest rates soared to 16.5% (we had a large loan!). On top of this, Alison, my wife, was pregnant with our first child. To cut a long story short, I was unable to handle this mentally and in effect, had a nervous breakdown.

I went for hypnotherapy, and spent a long time studying self help books. What I discovered was the secret to success both personally and organisationally.

The problem was not 'out there' with other people, the problem was with me and the way I saw the world, and this allowed my past problems to control my present.

So what? I hear you say. Well, if our past experience is not necessarily a great guide for us in life (and customer service), then what is? The answer is 'Principles'.

Principles rule everything

To use a simile, a principle is like a lighthouse. It doesn't move, it shows you the correct and safe way and if you don't take heed of it, you will end up on the rocks!

In his book, 'The 7 Habits of Highly Effective People', Stephen Covey tells a story similar to this:

> It was a dark and misty night and on the bridge of the Queen Mary 2, the first mate sees a light in his sea lane. He signals for it to move, but it will not, so he summons the captain from his cabin and says:
>
> "Captain, there is a light in our sea lane, and it will not move!"
>
> The captain replies: "Signal for it to move again."
>
> The first mate does this. "Move to starboard", he signals, and again the signal comes back,
>
> "Move to starboard yourself".
>
> The captain exclaims: "I can't believe this! Tell them who we are!"
>
> The first mate signals: "This is the Queen Mary 2, move to starboard!"
>
> The signal comes back: "This is the lighthouse … take your choice!"

This book is about customer service, so I don't propose to include more discussion and background on principles, but this chapter is about 'the principles of excellent customer service': i.e. what matters?

Put simply, we need to look at the roots of every individual and organisation. I give you this challenge. Answer these next two questions as quickly as you can.

1. Why am I here personally?
2. Why are we here organisationally?

Did you get a good answer, or is this quite hard?

Hard, I expect. (As the greatest minds ever known have been puzzling over these questions from time immemorial).

But we are only talking here about customer service, so the answer perhaps should look a bit like this.

- To be successful
- To make money

OK.

So what does this REALLY mean and how do we do it?

Please take a moment to write in the space below.

Let's take this one at a time.

1. What is success?

There are many definitions, but focusing on customer service, my view would be this:

Success is:-

- Finding an occupation that you love and
- Doing it to the best of your ability one day at a time

And the result of this will be: **outstanding customer service**. (The traditional western view of success, money and power, is far too shallow. However, it is likely that should you take the steps above, money and power will naturally follow, one way or the other).

2. How do we make money?

Well, as mentioned before, I suggest there are two simple ways to do this. Either work for a Mint or, double your prices and halve your costs.

Getting real and focusing on customer service, it seems to me that the best way to make money is by delivering a service that is so good, people are prepared to pay you for it. BOCS?

So now we are back to our customer service definition of success.

To deliver a service that is so good, people are prepared to pay you for it!

And the wonderful thing about this is that it's a natural equation:

The better the service, the more people are prepared to pay!

This raises some interesting questions:

Individually:

- Have I taken the time and effort to work out what I love doing?
- Or do I just work to pay the bills?
- Even if I can't or won't take the time and effort to work out what kind of work I love doing and more importantly, to organise myself to do it, have I got enough character and guts to give my best efforts to whatever it is I am doing at this time?

"If you can't be with the one you love, love the one you're with!"

Success really is about doing the best you can with what you have and what you are. It's not about money. So, bearing the above in mind:

- What would I want people to say about me at my funeral?
- And what do I need to change in order to achieve this?

I love the following quote from Jim Rohn:

"Work hard at your job, and you'll make a ….. living!
Work hard on yourself, and you make a …… success!"

Organisationally, it seems like Blindingly Obvious Common Sense that we're in business to deliver a service that is so good people are prepared to pay for it. So why, when asked the question "why are we in business" do we often get the answer 'to make money'? And why is it so hard to turn this Blindingly Obvious Common Sense into Blisteringly Normal Common Practice?

The reality of the situation is that it's a simple concept to deliver excellent customer service, but it's very hard to put it into practice.

To resolve this puzzle is the purpose of this book.

Success in making this work, relies upon everyone throughout an organisation being obsessive about great customer service no matter what their role or position. This can only be delivered by having an organisation with a Customer Focused Mission at its core and a management team that is:

- Personally obsessive about great service
- Personally turned on by their business
- Understand the magnitude of the task
- Have no hidden agenda
- Drive to make this difficult task seem easy

Somewhat rare. So, for this to really work inside any organisation, we need to know what matters to the organisation.

This can be found in two areas:

1. The things people say: The Mission statement (for further information on this, please see Appendix 1): This tells us 'what we're about'.

2. The actions that actually happen: This is when the 'Mission' gets put into practice.

And, of course, missions are always crystal clear, all personnel are passionately devoted to them at all levels and actions are always aligned to them.

Aren't they?

Are you sure?

If the Mission isn't there, or isn't clear or the actions aren't aligned, what does this tell us? And, more importantly how do we know **what matters**?

Even if the Mission is crystal clear and empowering to all, what happens when the behaviour isn't aligned? Actions speak louder than words, so we HAVE TO start off in any role, in any organisation, by knowing **what really matters**.

And this is rarely exceptional customer service on top of everything else!

If it isn't, it's hardly surprising that customer service is not delivered consistently and excellently in your organisation, department, or role. Other things will simply get in the way and the horse will get lost because it doesn't know where the water is.

For now, let's just explore the Mission of the organisation (and individual) a little further. We'll look at behaviour and why so often, it's not aligned with the Mission, later.

Please take some quality time to complete the exercise below. This will raise some vital questions about your organisation and you. These questions are rarely the ones that are addressed in Board meetings (or should I call them 'bored' meetings?), but we all know they are always the ones on the employees' lips outside all the meetings and official correspondence. So let's spend some time really getting this right.

Your organisation: What is the Mission of the organisation?

(Do I know? Is it clear? Does it help me and others do my job better? Especially when the going gets tough? If not, who do I need to speak to, or what else do I need to do?)

What is the 'Vision' that drives the 'Mission'?

What are the 'values' that ensure we deliver the 'Vision' through the 'Mission'?

How do these all relate to the customers' needs?

Is this all 'worthwhile' or am I beginning to have some doubts?

[The purpose of asking this 'worthwhile' question is simple. There is a basic human need to 'make a difference' or do something 'worthwhile' (note how many people work for charitable causes when they've become comfortable financially themselves). For many, the prime reason to work is one of survival and paying bills, but this will never produce excellence in customer service on its own. The ONLY way you can be sure of producing excellence in customer service is by having 'worthwhile' values and Mission. And this is what we want to find here].

OK, so it's dead easy to do this exercise on your organisation, to pick holes and ask pertinent questions (if you're not sure, just ask around at the coffee machine, you'll find the data you need very quickly), but how about doing this exercise on yourself?

Why bother? Well, the real issue is:

- Do you actually know your own 'Mission' and 'values' (it's much more likely that you know the second one than the first)?

- If so, have you spent time making sure it's aligned with those of your organisation? and

- If not, how will you know whether you're the right person to be generating excellent customer service in your organisation, at whatever level you find yourself?

Because if you don't / haven't / or can't, you will never enable the delivery of excellence in the long term.

So, have a go at this for you as an individual and your role in the organisation:

What is your Mission?

Individually	Your role in the organisation

(Do I know? Is it clear? Does it help me live and perform better? Especially when the going gets tough? If not, what else do I need to do?)

What is the 'Vision' that drives the 'Mission'?

Individually	Your role in the organisation

What are the 'values' that ensure we deliver the 'Vision' through the 'Mission'?

Individually	Your role in the organisation

And how, most importantly, do these all relate to the customers' needs?

Individually	Your role in the organisation

- Am I really spending my time on 'worthwhile' tasks?
- Do I often feel that I'm doing lots of things, but not really achieving a great deal?
- Do I feel that I have more talent and ability than my roles currently need or even allow?
- Is there a 'lighthouse' in my life when the storm comes?

If the answer to any of these is in doubt, you need to do some work here.

Circle of Concern vs. the Circle of Influence

The above exercises will hopefully have raised some very interesting (and vital) questions. To my knowledge, no-one ever said on their death bed:

- "I'm really glad I never did all that stuff that I really wanted to do".
- "Thank God, I never really fulfilled my potential".
- "I've got to live. I need to get back to that miserable job I spent so long complaining about and those back-stabbing turkeys I work with!"
- And the old chestnut: "I wish I'd spent more time at the office" (though I don't really think this is always true, as my suggestion is that you align your occupation with your passion, then spending more time in the office isn't always an issue - except perhaps to your loved ones!)

But you may well be tempted to say of the above exercises: "I don't set the 'Mission' or 'Vision' so there's precious little I can do to change it".

There may be some truth in this (we can't all be the CEO and even they have other people who dictate a lot of what they do), but remember you don't 'have to' do or think anything, so I urge you to consider this.

Everything we encounter in life can be split into two groups:

> GROUP ONE: things we're concerned about, but can't influence
> GROUP TWO : things we're concerned about and can influence

(Assuming that if we're not concerned about something, there's no point in spending any time on it either here, or elsewhere). So how do we approach this in a way that produces the results we want, and avoids frustration and stress?

Very simply, we do the following:

> GROUP TWO: We focus on this first. We have integrity, discipline and personal organisation, and we always (well, almost always - no-one's perfect!) do the best we can in this area. This means that we are effective in areas we can be and will, therefore, most likely be someone with some credibility.

> GROUP ONE: Assuming we do the things in group two as well as we can, then with the group one we do the following:

Sort it into two categories:

> Category 1: things we really have no influence on whatsoever (e.g. the weather and probably everything on the news). We accept this, spend as little time on it as possible and move on to something more worthy of our valuable time and attention.

> Category 2: things we might be able to have some indirect influence over (e.g.: someone else's decision, or even a 'Mission' and 'values').

Unfortunately, many people do exactly the opposite. They spend literally hours discussing, focusing on and moaning about something they have absolutely no influence on at all (just look at any web blog for ample evidence here) and just seem to have 'no time' to take some real pragmatic steps to influence things they can.

Let's call these people 'Normal'.

Truly effective and empowered people do exactly the opposite. They waste as little time as possible on the anything they have no influence over and spend the vast majority of their time and effort on finding solutions to the things that really matter.

Thomas Edison was a good example of this, in doing over 3000 experiments before he found a filament that worked in a light bulb (while all his friends urged him to give up and told him candles were 'fine'). [Note: beware the word 'fine'; it's that little devil that keeps you outside your circle of influence]. Other notable successful people who did this fantastically well include Gandhi, Nelson Mandela, Pierre Omidyar and Mother Theresa.

Let's call these people 'Abnormal'.

Now, let's just say you're the CEO of your organisation. Two people come to you with ideas for the 'Mission' and 'values'. One 'normal' and one 'abnormal'. Which are you going to listen to? This will depend on your attitude and mindset and the answer to this will basically be the answer to whether your organisation thrives or struggles.

Here's a diagram which influences this point:

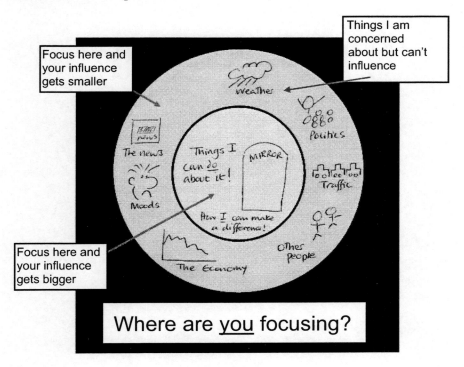

Basically, the more you focus on the things you can influence, the more things you'll be able to influence. Your 'circle of influence' will grow.

To quote the Chinese proverb:

"It is far better to strike a straight blow with a crooked stick than to spend your whole life trying to straighten the darn thing out!"

Not only does this improve results dramatically and organisationally, but also it makes life more fun and meaningful!

Here are some top tips to help you 'strike straight blows' with your 'crooked stick'!

Things to do more of:

- Spending time on your own Mission and values.
- Goal setting.
- Proper planning (time management).
- Relationship building.
- Reading and learning.
- Getting feedback.
- Giving feedback: with courage and consideration.
- Using 'I' messages when giving feedback, e.g. avoid 'you're lazy' and instead say 'I feel hurt when you don't help me with the chores'. It's MUCH easier to do and more effective.
- Effective influencing of things that matter.
- Having fun.
- Being a human 'being' not a human 'doing'.

Things to do less of:

- Watching or reading the news (good news is bad news and bad news is good news - do you really need a dose of this every day?).
- Tip: buy a weekly 'news roundup' magazine and read that instead.
- Excessive TV / Internet / Gaming.
- Tip: do a bit, but be very selective and disciplined, otherwise it will take over your life. Everything in (planned) moderation.
- Tip: avoid 'soaps' and 'reality TV' unless this really is central to the purpose of your life (can it be?).
- Moaning: just don't, it's destructive to you and those around you - and no-one takes any notice of a 'moaner'.
- Using the phrases:
  - 'That makes me'
  - 'I can't'
  - 'I have to'
  - 'I don't have time'
- Talking about other people in a negative way - this says more about you than it does about them!
- Anything that you have absolutely no influence over - because it's just S.A.D. Stressful, Annoying and Disastrous!

So now we know where we should focus and ways of avoiding stress and pointlessness, here are some principles to guide you in what you do choose to do with your time. These will all be within your circle of influence.

Further principles of excellent customer service (and life):

- Habits dictate actions.
- Treat your neighbour as you would like to be treated (if you were them).
- 'Shift' happens.
- Attitude is more important that aptitude.
- What you appreciate, appreciates.
- Actions speak louder than words.
- Customers are people (with needs desires and frustrations just the same as you).
- No one is trying to do a bad job: in fact,
- Everyone is trying to do their best.

1. Habits dictate actions:

We all have habits (my wife says I have more than anyone else): some are very helpful - like opening doors for people, and looking people in the eyes when speaking to them. Some are not - like being so wrapped up in our own world that we forget to say hello to someone, or not noticing the fact our wife has had her hair done.

Habits are the root of everything. Habits have been learned over a lifetime and are very hard to break.

Old habits will always be with us: we cannot 'change a habit', we can only form new habits that we choose to make more powerful than the old ones, so they override them. This is uncomfortable, and can take a while.

For example, if you are wearing a watch, please take it off and put it on the other wrist. How does it feel? Is the strap comfortable? Is the hole in the right place?

Depending on your motivation and mindset, it can take a micro second or a lifetime to change a habit. I know people who have, one day, just stopped smoking, because they changed their mindset overnight. I also know people who have struggled all their lives to give up and still haven't succeeded.

A basic rule would be, if you can do something consistently for three weeks, you're likely to be able to form a new habit of it. So it's not too hard, but it does take commitment.

A habit is formed from three factors:

- Knowledge: the mental ability to do something.
- Skill: the tools to do it.
- Attitude: the desire to do it (lots of work on this subject in this book, but this is basically up to you. If you don't want to change any habits and really put some effort into becoming great at customer service, then please stop reading now and turn back to 'Hello' magazine. It will be a better use of your time!).

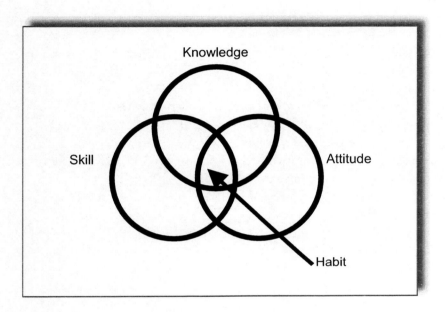

A new habit can only be formed when all three factors are present:

For example: a teenage child may have the knowledge to tidy up his or her room and he or she may have the ability to do it, but often the attitude is missing!

Conversely, he or she may have the desire to drive a car, but may not have the knowledge or skill. It can't be a habit in either instance.

Most training and development works almost exclusively on the 'knowledge' and 'skill' area, in the naïve belief that it will then get done. The truth, as we all know as recipients, is that without the attitude, NOTHING will change. The room will stay untidy and the customer will stay fed up.

You can take a horse to water, but you can't make it drink.

Training and development MUST start with 'attitude' and later cover 'skills' and 'knowledge'. Otherwise it's a non-starter. You must have a thirsty horse before you take it to the water if you want the water to actually be drunk.

Conversely, if the attitude is there, the horse will search and search until it finds water, the customer will be happy and the room will miraculously find a way to become clean.

Here are some great customer service habits in the form of a simple checklist:

INDIVIDUAL:

- Answering the phone promptly.
- Asking for permission before putting the customer on hold.
- Avoiding jargon and putting things in a way that's easy for the customer to understand.
- Seeking clarification from the customer in order to correctly understand his or her needs.
- Showing genuine concern and interest, in voice and body language.
- Suggesting intelligent options and alternatives, when you can't deliver what's been asked for.
- Focusing on one thing at a time so that it gets done properly.
- Looking people in the eye when speaking to them.
- Valuing feedback.
  - From the customer.
  - Internally.
  - From other stakeholders (e.g. Suppliers).
- Leading by example.
- Apologising sincerely for mistakes.
- Remaining calm and understanding when dealing with problems.
- Having a watertight system for returning calls.
- Following-up after issues have been resolved.
- Viewing complaints as an opportunity to excel and improve, not as a waste of valuable time.
- Effective use of email (a subject in itself)
- Effective use of answer machine/voicemail.
- Knowing how your role affects the front line.
- Showing appreciation when colleagues do a good job.
- Viewing all stakeholders as customers.

ORGANISATIONAL:

- Systems that enable your people to do things well including computer systems designed to get to the right information quickly and with little fuss.
- Training people so they know how to use systems properly.
- Training people in service attitude as well as roles.
- Surveying customers regularly.
- Collecting data on aspects of service that are measurable (e.g. telephone waiting times, on time deliveries etc).
- Acting on the results of the data to improve.
- Having a watertight complaints system.
- Training everyone in personal organisation.
- Surveying employees.
- Collecting and making available data on the bottom line effects of poor service.
- Regular departmental or group meetings to keep everyone informed of changes and developments, and how it affects service.
- Internal communications (e.g. newsletter) focused on customer service excellence.
- An induction that looks at everything from the point of view of its affect on service.
- A constant focus on how to reduce bureaucracy and obstacles.
- Promotion prospects based on attitude and service, rather than just skills.
- Open communication across all levels and departments, no politics.
- Formal and informal recognition of great service.
- Making and interpreting policies around the needs of the customer over and above the needs of the 'system'.
- Having a process that enables policies to be changed to improve customer service.
- Checks and balances to ensure standards of appearance and service.

- Customer service at the forefront of job descriptions and staff reviews.
- Work parties to continually review service and how to improve it.
- Taking disciplinary action where service consistently falls below the level required.
- Publicising examples of excellent service to colleagues.
- Having a system for senior management (and sticking to it) to regularly meet with customers.
- Putting posters on walls about the importance of great service.
- A culture of constant innovation: 'Our job is to make our existing services obsolete before our competitors do'.

And here are some awful ones

- Being disorganised.
- Leaving phones ringing.
- Leaving unclear or out of date messages on your answer machine so no one knows where you are or how to get hold of you.
- Transferring and putting calls on hold with no reference to the customer.
- Using jargon and getting frustrated when customers don't understand you or the issue you're dealing with.
- Jumping to conclusions without finding out the full information.
- Being resentful of 'wasted' time, and showing it in your voice and body language.
- Avoiding suggesting alternatives and taking a 'jobsworth' attitude.
- Trying to do too many things at the same time.
- Avoiding eye contact when speaking to people.
- Avoiding responsibility: 'It's not my fault'.
- Rejecting feedback.
- Not leading by example: Telling others to do what you don't do (e.g. returning calls on time).
- Avoiding apologising wherever possible.
- Getting annoyed and frustrated when dealing with problems.
- Not returning calls ('If it's important, they'll phone back'!).
- Not following-up on issues as appropriate.
- Resenting complaints.
- Ineffective use of email (a subject in itself).
- Having no idea how your role affects the front line ('I just work here'!).
- Never thanking others.
- Having a cynical view of customers, viewing them as 'only the customer' (and thinking how much easier your job would be without them).

Challenge yourself: Tick the ones you're good at and give yourself a pat on the back, then make sure you have a SYSTEM that ensures they always will happen going forward.

For example: I used to travel very long distances for work when my children were young. I used to rush home when I could in order to catch the children before they went to bed, but by the time I got there, I was exhausted and grumpy (and not much of a father).

Sometimes, however, I got it right and I learned that the way to do this was to stop when I got out of the car and ask myself, 'What would a GREAT father do when he walked through the front door?' And then I'd do it. It worked a treat, so now I try to do this every time I face a difficult issue (and with three boys, that's a lot of times) with my children.

Tick the ones you're bad at, but don't beat yourself up about them. Ask yourself:

- What is one thing that I could change in the next three weeks?
- And then the next three weeks etc.
- Who else could help me and hold me accountable?

(Remember, stick to three weeks because it's generally recognised that this is the amount of time it takes to form a new habit). Challenge those close to you. Ask them to do the same exercise and repeat it every six months. Most training and development programmes have almost NO IMPACT because there's no action. The key to success is to have simple systemised steps to create the action.

Don't think about it.

Do it.

Now!

2. Treat your neighbour as you would like to be treated (if you were them).

This is the 'golden rule' to all human interaction and the basis of all religion. It sounds very soft and cuddly and very selfless. In an odd way, it's exactly the opposite. The law of attraction states that if we do this, it will be done unto us!

I've added the extra bit in brackets because the key to this is to understand your customer. I'd be delighted as a customer if I walked into a mobile phone shop and they showed me the simplest plainest phone that just made phone calls (that would be a novel invention don't you think?), but I think that my needs and desires might not be typical of their clientele.

So how do we do this?

This is the complicated bit: We have to ask them!

But this is more than the lame 'can I help you?' It's more like an internal conversation that goes a bit like this:

- My role is to generate sales.

- The best way I can do this is to REALLY understand the customer and his or her needs.

- What I personally need or desire for myself is completely irrelevant to this transaction - and so is my ego.

- That way I can:
    - help those I can help quickly and efficiently,
    - redirect those I can't help quickly and efficiently, thus not wasting either of our time and generating trust and a positive relationship.

- Have a happy and rewarding day, no matter what the outcome.

This is how I'd like someone to deal with me if I were the customer - wouldn't you?

Amazingly, people who actually do this consistently and excellently always seem to generate the most sales and have the most loyal customers - odd isn't it!

The more you focus on your needs, the less of them you'll get. The more you focus on your customers' needs, the more of your own you'll get.

And, by the way, you'll have a fulfilling life at the same time.

Note: This extends not only on a personal basis when talking, but in any form of communication, for example signage or advertising.

Here are some examples of what I mean.

I recently visited a stately home with friends on a day out. While walking in the gardens, every twenty feet or so there was a sign staked in the ground stating 'Keep Off The Grass'. My friend pointed out that the message really annoyed him, "Why don't they put 'Please'?" I thought about it for a second and took it one stage further, "Please Keep Off The Grass, Many Thanks". Again, blindingly obvious - it immediately portrays a sense of calm and appreciation.

I am sure like me you were taught at an early age to think before you speak, but were not told to think before you do most things. We all know the "no bloody nothing" pub or restaurant. Many pubs and restaurants have signs effectively saying, 'don't annoy me', or 'customers are a pain and I can't be bothered to talk to them'. Recognise some of these?

- No responsibility accepted for your car in car park.
- Do not park on the grass.
- No children over 10 on the play equipment.
- Parents are responsible for their children.
- Only food purchased here to be consumed in the garden.
- No Parking in front of these garage doors.
- No smoking.
- No alcohol sold to under 18's.
- No tobacco sold to under 18's.
- No children under 14 allowed in the bar.
- No cheques cashed.
- No food after 2.00pm.
- Behave yourself, we are part of Pub Watch.

Do the words 'Industrial Age Mindset' spring to mind? And do we just get back into our cars as customers and go somewhere else when we see all this nonsense?

3. 'Shift' happens:

They were smart in the 60's weren't they? When teaching this in front of live audiences, I have to be more careful with my words and say "expect the unexpected".

I remember a common phrase used in the UK leisure industry:

"This would be a great business if it wasn't for the customer!"

This attitude is hardly likely to engender great service and happy customers. In fact it will become a 'self- fulfilling prophecy'.

The reality is that

Customers are NOT always right
They are often grumpy, difficult and obtuse
But they *are* still the customer!

Customers can make life difficult, deliveries can get lost, computers can break down and sometimes it rains on a Monday morning. It's called LIFE!

If we choose to deal with this resentfully, we'll reap what we sow. If we choose to meet all obstacles as 'just the way it is, so let's see how we can make it better', then we'll reap what we sow. It's our choice.

Life is simply a journey and it throws all sorts of obstacles in our way. Success is judged in the way we meet and get over these obstacles. I think it's as simple as that.

Some examples:

- Did Thomas Edison give up after experiment number 2999?
- Did James Dyson give up with his bagless vacuum cleaner when he was repeatedly turned down for funding?
- Did Nelson Mandela give up during his 26 years in jail?

Or did all these people accept the obstacles and move on to finding solutions within their circle of influence?

Some ideas:

- See obstacles as 'opportunities to impress your customer and learn more about your business'.

- See difficult customers as 'people who are unhappy and who may need some help'.

- When someone asks "how are you?", try replying "great", "excellent", or "fabulous", instead of "not bad"! You never know, it may come true!

- When all this happens say "how fascinating" or "how interesting" and then get to work on it.

- (The use of language is VERY important. If we speak to ourselves and say something is a 'problem', we'll be right. If we speak to ourselves and say it's an 'opportunity', we'll be right. Our brains make what we tell them into reality for us).

- Rename your alarm clock, your 'opportunity clock' (with thanks to Zig Zigar). OK this may be a bridge too far, but you get the picture!

4. Attitude is more important than aptitude

As customers we all know this, yet when we are dealing with our own customers we tend to forget this. Why is this? The ego gets in the way. "I don't want to risk not knowing the answer, or I'm scared that you might even say 'no', so I end up not phoning you".

We are all like overgrown kids, we just want to be cared for and treated well. As your customer, if your attitude is great, I don't really mind if you can't give me the best price or the latest gadget, I'll do business with you because I like you. I'll like you if I trust you.

It's really very simple. That's often why it's hard to do.

There are so many people now who are so expertly focused on particular specialisms in their line of business, that they almost forget why they're there:

To deliver a service that is so good
People are prepared to pay you for it!

Most customers don't expect everything to go right first time every time, they don't expect everything to be in stock and they don't expect you to have the answers to everything they can dream up to catch you out. They just want you to care.

How do you do this? Some tips:

- Treat them with courtesy and respect.
- Persist in finding out their real needs and their 'desired result'.
- Tell them the TRUTH always, including the drawbacks of your different products or services.
- Tell them when things have gone wrong and go out of your way to put them right as quickly as possible.
- Tell them some of the issues they may encounter and how to overcome them. Educate them, you're the expert, they just want you to help them.
- Confront reality: Tell them when you don't know the answer and what you're going to do about it.
- Keep commitments: for example by phoning them back when you say you will (if you just do this, you'll be in the top 20%).
- Deliver the results they expect, plus that extra little bit.

In a nutshell: be honest, be caring, and manage their expectations. The rest will take care of itself.

Here's an example of what not to do. I call this the "Lassie Approach".

You walk into a bar, a petrol station, or a newsagent and the person behind the counter rests their 'paws' on the counter. They then lift their head in an upwards movement as if their shirt collar was a little tight. This initial action is their way of saying 'good morning, how can I help you?'

You place your order/ request and in total silence they get what you want, place it on the counter and say how much. You pay them, they cash up. That's it.

If you think about it, you will agree it's like having been served by "Lassie". No courtesy, no interaction and you're left guessing!

5. What you appreciate, appreciates:

This is one of today's real hot topics. Only as I was writing this, did I receive an invitation to attend a seminar in London proudly proclaiming that it was 'the only seminar in the world today on the law of attraction'. A great claim, but probably not entirely true. The point of this principle is that it really is 'blindingly obvious common sense', however, so often in today's world it isn't common practice. The other way of putting this is: 'what you focus on expands'.

So:

If you only appreciate profit: you'll get short term profit (usually at the expense of long-term customer service).

If you appreciate service: you'll get good service (sometimes at the expense of short term profits).

The real questions are:

- Is your organisation really geared up to deliver excellent service, even if it is at the expense of short-term profits?

- Or, when push comes to shove, will the powers that be throw your customer service out of the window to make the month end figures work?

6. Actions speak louder than words.

You may recall from your childhood the story of the goose that laid the golden egg. In this story, a poor farmer owns a goose, which one day lays a golden egg. It continues to do this until the farmer becomes fabulously wealthy.

Initially, the farmer is hugely grateful and looks after the goose with expert care and attention, but after a while, becomes greedy and stops looking after the goose so well. Eventually, his basic instincts get the better of him. He chops the head off the goose in order to get all the golden eggs at once, only to find that there are none inside.

So it is with customer service: that goose is the organisation and all its stakeholders. The golden egg is the profits and long-term health of the organisation. Obviously one has to look after, cherish and nurture the goose, in order for it to continue to thrive and lay more and more golden eggs.

It's really easy to look after the goose when she's laying golden eggs. The question we need to search our souls (and ask all our stakeholders) is :

- Do we have the courage and determination to stick by the goose and keep feeding and looking after her when she goes through a barren patch, and the eggs are temporarily less plentiful?

- Or will we, like so many organisations (especially those who answer to short-term shareholders above all else), lop her pretty head off and reach inside.

The golden eggs are the results of excellent customer service from your organisation. Unless the goose is happy and healthy in ALL areas, she cannot lay golden eggs consistently and excellently. Very often the smallest things show this up in an organisation and in service. Very often the small things are big issues.

As customers:

- We don't care if you're the cheapest if you're painful to deal with.
- We don't care if you're the fastest if you're not accurate.
- And we don't care if you're the most innovative if you're not 'caring' in every little detail of every transaction every day.

7. Customers are people (with needs desires and frustrations just the same as you):

Here is a breakthrough - Customers are people!

But you wouldn't think it when considering the way some people treat them. The point of this principle is that life [and customer service] is not just about profits.

If we treat the people well, the profits will follow.

I think every organisation who deals in service should have this as their Mission. It will guide and empower all those who work for the organisation, but it will only work if they really mean it and all people in the organisation at all levels actually stick to it and do it no matter what.

In a training program that I teach, I ask people to imagine that they are on their death bed with 5 minutes left, and their friends and family are at their bedside! The question is this, what would they want to say to them?

Here are some ideas of things that have never come up:

- At least I made budget.
- I did some great deals, and really screwed those suckers.
- Thank God I was able to buy that BMW with the bonus I got by manipulating the figures.

A true story:

> Four people visited a pub for Sunday lunch. Three ordered pork and the third ordered beef. When the staff served up the food to the table, she plonked them down and left. The person who ordered the beef had got pork - the same as the other three. The customer sent for the member of staff and explained that he had ordered beef.
>
> He was told that he had beef on his plate. This argument went back and forth, until the customer said:
>
> "Well if it's beef, why is there apple sauce on the plate?"
>
> The member of staff just sighed and took the plate away.
>
> You have to ask why a staff member would want to deal with the issue in this way. It makes no sense at all.

"What do we live for if it is not to make life less difficult for each other", so spake George Elliot and although this again seems like BOCS, it is actually rather profound, for if this is not what life is for, then what is it for? We cannot take our shiny cars and large houses with us, so why do we spend so much effort trying to acquire them?

Ironically, if we turn conventional wisdom on it's head, and do spend our time REALLY focusing on giving great service NO MATTER WHAT because CUSTOMERS ARE PEOPLE (with needs and desires like us), then the other things tend to follow because:

We are in business:

To deliver a service that is so good
People are prepared to pay you for it!

And

The better the service
The more people are prepared to pay

Ironic isn't it?

8. No one is trying to do a bad job:

Belief in this is an absolute MUST. But, when faced with the Sunday lunch scenario quoted above, it's often a very difficult belief to support.

So often, when delivering training, I ask the questions:

1. Why do people do a bad job?

2. Why are customers difficult?

So come on, you have a go at answering them (put down 3 or 4 answers for each one), and then I'll tell you my point:

1. Why do people do a bad job?

2. Why are customers difficult?

Now, have a look at your answers, and see how many contain the word 'they'? Is it most of them? If so, this point is crucial, because if it is, you probably don't agree with this point.

For question 1: my belief is that no one gets out of bed each morning determined to make a pigs ear of the day and everyone's life a misery. So the issue to determine is, why does it really happen? And the only way you (or anyone else) can determine this, is by asking them!

Assuming they are not trying to do a bad job, your objective in asking them why is to find out the real issue:

- Are there processes stopping them?
- Are the systems OK?
- Do they need input from someone else?
- Do they need training?
- Are they in the wrong job?
- Or are they just having a bad day?
- Or do they have personal issues?

In other words: 'What's REALLY stopping the horse from having the drink?' Because we all know, it's BOCS that horses need to drink to survive. So, if they're not drinking, it's possible that they might not be thirsty, but surely it's more probable that there's something else getting in the way? We cannot resolve the issues at the same level of thinking we were at when we created them.

So, in order to resolve these issues, properly, for the long term benefit of all parties, you need to understand the real cause of the issue. So you can **address the cause, not the symptom.**

Taking the scenarios above:

- If we assume that the person delivering the bad service is doing it because they're a bozo, we'll address this as the issue, and make a dog's dinner of the whole situation (as so often happens). This will result in a negative outcome all round. The managers will lose because they haven't addressed the issue and so it will happen again. The deliverer of the bad service will lose because the issue won't have been resolved and he/she will be left feeling unfulfilled and the organisation will lose as a result of all of this. As for the customer, he/she has received the bad service and so will probably spread the bad news to friends and family and certainly won't go back for more!

- If we take the time to ask the right questions, with empathy and focus, we'll get to the cause and be able to address it properly and effectively, producing a win / win outcome!

It just takes time, courage, and consideration. Unfortunately these are often in scarce supply ... but at least you now know!

As for customers being difficult ... surely not? We'll deal with them in a later chapter, so you'll have to read on or skip a bit. It depends on what your personal CFM directs you to do.

The cost and opportunity of great or poor customer service.

There is, of course, no hard and fast rule in this area, so the cost and opportunity of customer service (great or poor) in your organisation will be a matter for you to consider and come to a conclusion upon. However, I can give you some good common sense guidelines based on extensive research, personal knowledge, and consultancies I've carried out with service companies.

This subject could rightly deserve any chapter of its own as there is a huge amount of research and data available in this area. However, as usual it's all common sense and this book is designed to try and keep things fun and simple, to help you achieve real change consistently and easily.

Type of Business	Rough cost multiple of gaining a new customer vs. retaining an existing one
Grocer	6
Brand Manager	8
Restaurant	12
Holiday Park	50
Property Owner	200+

All the research that I have conducted indicates some startling and hugely important figures in the following six key issues:

- The cost of winning new customers versus retaining existing ones.
- The number of people customers typically tell about poor service (versus great service).
- The cost of delivering poor service.
- The opportunity of delivering great service.
- The 'lifetime value' of a customer.
- The amount of people who say they are 'satisfied' at the time when they change supplier.

So, to take these in turn:

1. The cost of winning new customers versus retaining existing ones.

Research indicates very strongly and common sense backs this up, that it is more expensive to win a new customer than to retain an existing one. Here are some guidelines:
Please note: these figures are rough guidelines based upon my experience only. Every organisation is different.

The point here is threefold:

- Firstly: It costs a huge amount more to find a new customer than to look after an existing one. So why do so many organisations have a huge sales and marketing budget, but are reluctant to spend money on customer service analysis, training, systems and measurement, when this type of investment should return a minimum of six times the investment made in the previously mentioned area?

- Secondly: You need to do your homework. The way to organise this is to look at your organisation's level and costs of customer turnover honestly. So many organisations have massive hidden costs created by unacceptable levels of customer turnover that they just regard as a normal overhead.

- Thirdly: It is not free to deliver excellent customer service. You have to invest time and resources to make it happen. It won't happen by luck. But it is much more cost effective to invest here than in sales and marketing. You just have to have faith and know the right things to do!

You may need the help of an outside consultant to look at these. I know the word 'consultant' is a rude word, but they really can add value to your organisation if they are experts in this area and not in your business. This is because they will not see your situation as 'normal' but will look at everything objectively. When you've done this, look at how much it would really cost to delight your customers consistently - then compare the cost and benefit of the two!

My bet is that this would perhaps call for some up-front investment, but going forward, would be a relatively small cost compared to the amount you're currently spending on sales, marketing and hidden costs of customer turnover.

The good news is that this exercise will:

- Decrease the cost of sales and marketing
- Decrease hidden overheads, and
- Improve customer spend and profit margins

Thus having a huge impact on your bottom line.

Then you can reinvest some of the money you've saved from this into business generation with your other existing customers and get the flywheel of your business turning faster and faster.

In fact, if you invest 1/6th of the amount you saved in improving your customer service, you're in line to benefit by 5 or 6 times the amount on your bottom line as minimum, but depending on your business, the impact could be substantially more.

If you don't believe me, here's some research from the Brookeside Group.

Brookeside Group research shows that companies can boost profit by as much as 85% by focusing on client retention. Why? Increasing the loyalty of customers by as little as 1% has the same impact as reducing operating costs by as much as 10%.

And here's a simple one from American Express.

Consumers are willing to pay an average of 36% more for a decent pub meal if the service, food and atmosphere are of a high standard.

So, a challenge: It's easy to boost bottom line profits by slashing costs, but the real test of guts, faith and genius is to take the other, less direct and much harder route. This is the route that gives the 'great' results.

2. The number of people customers typically tell about 'poor' service (versus 'great' service)

This figure is all guesswork, however, it is consistent guesswork that repeats itself time and time again at my seminars. In a nutshell:

We tell two or three people about a 'great' customer experience
We tell <u>everyone</u> about a 'poor' one

It's just human nature. We are all basically insecure and the best way to deal with that is to focus on the things that everyone else gets wrong rather than address the plank in our own eye! (It's called focusing on the circle of concern, rather than the circle of influence, and your poor customers may not have read this wonderful book and so will still be stuck there).

Just watch the news, or any reality television if you don't believe me.

The impact of this of course is substantial:

- If we delight a customer, they will tell one or two people. However, we all know that this relatively small number will actually be quite impactful on our business. As customers ourselves, we are not often overwhelmed with great customer service, so when one of our friends tells us about something 'great' that we are likely to be interested in (because otherwise our friends wouldn't be talking to us about it), we are quite likely to also become customers of that organisation. For instance: how many times have we tried a restaurant or a hotel because we've been recommended it?

- If we let a customer down with bad service, their insecurity and upset means that they probably won't tell us, but they'll tell (and put off) everyone else they know (and many that they don't). This is how businesses fail overnight.

Nine out of ten people don't complain
They just go elsewhere and tell all their friends to do the same

But worse still, the people who hear it secondhand will probably tell a few people about it themselves, even though they've never even done business with you!

Bad news is good news, and it travels fast!

So, get this right and you'll build your business steadily and with very low costs.

Get it wrong and you could kill your business almost overnight depending on the value of 'word of mouth' in your business.

- Word of mouth is very likely to be high in businesses based almost entirely on service as their brand, and customer spend being discretionary rather than essential (for example a holiday resort, restaurant or hotel).

- Word of mouth value will be lower in a brand based business, for example a company like Coca-Cola, however, even they believe that excellence in this area is essential.

- Word of mouth value may be hugely important in a specialist and essential area, for example a lawyer or accountant.

- This really becomes a hot potato for monopolies: so often we hear about word of mouth for monopolies (particularly in politics and in state monopolies). If they do not get their customer service right, or make real effort to be market focused, as soon as the monopoly begins to break down, the organisation will fall like a pack of cards because it has been built on sand.

- We see this happening very often in politics, where for example, a politician stands out against sleaze whilst embezzling their expenses, or has an affair with an office assistant whilst extolling the virtues of family values! If the customer feels abused, and not valued they will abandon an organisation like rats from a sinking ship.

And remember, the world is changing at a massively fast pace. The Internet is empowering the customer unlike anything before - the quicker business heads recognise this, the more likely it is that their business will thrive going forward.

3. The cost of delivering poor service

Again, many studies have been conducted in this area. I find research commissioned by Coca-Cola particularly interesting, which concluded that organisations who fail to deliver customer service can in effect be spending up to 40% of operations budget on dealing with the issues that are raised as a result.

Of course this is completely unsustainable, yet, so often, this becomes the case because the organisation has either been a monopoly, has been at the cutting edge in its field, or has expanded quickly but has not addressed customer service proactively and will usually see itself disappearing as fast as it appeared.

When AOL launched its free Internet service, it hadn't invested in the infrastructure to deal with the deluge of customer demand that the offer created. The poor service that customers experienced, effectively nullified the benefit of the offer. An expensive mistake! And remember, customers have VERY long memories.

4. The opportunity of delivering great service

Warwick Business School in the UK, analysed companies' figures on a like for like basis, by splitting them into two categories ('above average' customer service and 'below average' customer service).

The results were of course BOCS:

- Above average customer service companies averaged about **50% higher** levels of turnover than below average customer service companies.
- When this was translated to net profit it was almost **double** on average.
- When this was translated to 'return on total assets', they found this was **three times as good** in the 'good' companies.

Isn't it marvellous when someone takes the time and effort to give a statistic that proves what we already know is BOCS? Turnover will be higher because there will be:

- More customers
- Buying more things
- Often at higher prices

Net profit will be higher because:

- The turnover is higher
- The costs are lower
- The margins are better

Return on total assets will be higher because:

- Net profit is higher
- Innovation is higher
- Expensive motivational overheads and brand building expenses are not required
- Staff motivation and retention is higher

5. The 'lifetime value' of a customer

This is a simple but powerful exercise that I get people to do in our seminars.

Spend five minutes on this now and see how your mindset changes about how much each individual customer is worth to your business. Because, when you are risking this amount of money every time you interact with them, it's highly likely that you'll see this as a much bigger risk (and opportunity) than you ever considered before, and you'll make sure that systems, processes and behaviour measures are aligned to achieving consistency and excellence as standard, all day every day. Whether you are there or not!

Please fill in this simple table in round figures, and then do the maths to get the final figure.

The lifetime value of my average customer:

A	Average customer spend per visit	
B	Average visits per lifetime	
C	Total average customer value (A X B)	
D	Number of people recommended by this customer (if we are consistently excellent)	
E	Multiply by average customer value (C)	
F	Total average recommended customer value (D X E)	
G	Total lifetime value of an average customer (C + F)	

Now you've done this, get everyone in your group, department or organisation to do the same. Then have a meeting to discuss the process and the figures it produced. You'll be amazed at the progress and mindset change you get. Then speak to your boss about this, then get him or her to do the same.

Then contact us: we can help you get this right! And from the figure you'll have, you'll know why it's so crucial to get it right!

6. The amount of people who say they are 'satisfied' at the time when they change supplier.

Again, BOCS, but this time surprisingly little research. We all know as customers, that if we are merely 'satisfied' with a product or service, we will:

- Not be loyal to that product or service
- Not tell anyone else to use them
- Probably keep our 'eye out' (either consciously or sub consciously for an alternative supplier).

There is a wonderful book on this particular point by Ken Blanchard called 'Raving Fans'. It makes this point clearly and in a fun and simple manner (it also has a lot of interesting stories). The point he makes is this:

'Satisfied' customers are not enough; you need 'raving fans'.

We know this from our own experiences:

- When we are just 'satisfied' by a restaurant, we will go somewhere else next time, and
- When our friends ask us 'what's it like?', we'll say 'OK, but not worth going out of your way for'.
- When we've dealt with a lawyer who did the job but treated us adequately, we'll look for another one next time.
- When our accountant does the job, but little else, we'll ask our friends what their accountant is like.

So why, when we get to work do we:

- Think that 'satisfied' is 'good enough'?
- Measure (and proudly publish) customer 'satisfaction' figures?
- Go on courses and implement systems to produce customer 'satisfaction'?
- Ask in a restaurant if everything was 'OK'?

We don't want things to be 'OK'!!!

They have to be 'great', or they're 'poor'

It's as simple as that.

I think that the worst experience I have had in this area indelibly etched in my mind, was when I was working for a company that made a lot of deliveries. I was in the operations department and the organisation had just undergone a 'seamless transition' in its delivery service (never believe anyone when they tell you something will be 'seamless': it never is, so they'd serve you much better as an internal customer if they were honest with you, told you the issues that might occur, told you where to go for help if they did, and asked you to feedback issues to help them improve during the transition). When dealing with a poor delivery service issue, I was told by the transport manager: *"We're no worse than anyone else!"*

The sad thing was that he thought that this was OK!

And, of course, he is not alone: How many times has a service provider asked you,

"Is everything OK?" I imagine 85% of the time. And what is the answer we give, 100% of the time? "Yes it's OK". The provider is happy, the customer service box has been ticked. The fact there has been no real feedback and that the customer has merely said "It's ok" seems immaterial.

I bet if you bought the latest Ferrari, the day after you picked it up the salesman would call to ask you 'if you were really happy with it, was it a joy to drive, was all the paperwork in order and was there anything else the dealership could do to help?' Not 'Is everything OK?'

Here is some information to back this point up:

The Brookeside Group:

> *"If you are not investing in loyalty, you are working too hard. In today's competitive business environment, companies must learn that customer satisfaction isn't enough. Retaining and nurturing client relationships and building loyalty, should be an essential component of any company's growth strategy."*

A study in the early 1980's for Coca-Cola concluded (among other things) that, up to:

80% of customers are 'satisfied' at the point when they leave.

I'm not sure how I can emphasise this point enough. This is VITAL. If you only remember and act on a few things from this book, this is one of them!

'Satisfied' customers are not good enough!
You're either 'great' or 'poor'

Whilst this has always been the case, it is becoming more and more important in this world of massive change. The Internet is empowering the customer unlike anything before it. Customers can research competitors and switch at the 'drop of a hat'. Advertising and marketing is losing its influence. Customers can feedback on organisations on websites that all the world can see. Third World students are learning English and have a fantastic customer service mentality. The power base of the world is shifting East, and the writing is on the wall for the West.

The ONLY way to long term profitability is customer delight!

So, MDs, FDs, Accountants and Managers, switch your spend today. Spend less on sales and marketing, spend more on customer service! Everyone else, switch your focus today. Spend less time on trivia and procedure and more time on developing yourself and delivering great service every day.

To Conclude:

- Principles govern life.
- Why are we here if it is not to deliver service to others?
- Why deliver an 'OK' service when you can deliver great service?
- And if we take notice of and do all this, then we'll be happy and rich (in whatever form of currency that's important to us!).

I leave this chapter with an article from CNN, and a quote from Gandhi (that seems to fit!)

Coca-Cola installed its 1-800-GET-COKE lines in late 1983 to promote feedback. Roger Nunley, manager of industry and consumer affairs at Coca-Cola USA, says some studies indicated that only one unhappy person in 50 takes time to complain.

"The other 49 switch brands, so it just makes good business sense to seek them out," he says. Without the toll-free lines, Coca-Cola might never have understood the depths of its error in trying to replace old Coke with new. Right after the Company launched its reformulated New Coke in 1985, calls on the phone system fizzed from an average of 400 a day to more than 12,000.

Nine out of ten were from customers who said they preferred the old cola to the new drink. On the day following old Coke's return as Coca-Cola Classic, 18,000 people called, including thousands who had complained earlier. They wanted to say thank you. Nunley says that consumer 'emotion' -- his term for brand loyalty -- is stronger today for Coke Classic than it was before the episode. And by selling both Cokes and several new colas, the Company has increased its U.S. market share to over 40%.

"The best way to find yourself is to use yourself in the service of others." Mahatma Gandhi.

Chapter Four: What gets in the way?

"Of all tyrannies, a tyranny exercised for the good of its victims may be the most oppressive. It may be better to live under robber barons than under omnipotent moral busybodies. The robber baron's cruelty may sometimes sleep, his cupidity may at some point be satiated; but those who torment us for our own good will torment us without end, for they do so with the approval of their own conscience." C S Lewis

How true is that today? We all know that it makes no sense in the long run to break the law and promote dysfunctionality, yet prisons are at record levels and legislation is rampant. We all know it's BOCS to deliver great customer service, yet, so often it just fails to happen. So why is this? This is the second great question this book was written to answer.

When I was researching this book and preparing for training courses, I would read and go to seminars, which all made perfect sense. But in the end, I felt no wiser. The issue was that they made too much sense: "It's a good idea to deliver great customer service". We all know this and we all know how to look people in the eye when speaking to them, phone them back when promised and treat them with courtesy and respect. It's BOCS. The real question is: **why isn't it common practice?**

My view is that this was the great unanswered question in customer service and if I could answer this, then this book would really empower you the reader, to actually go out and change something, so that you can start delighting your customers. Because:

Words without action are nothing!

Any psychologist worth his or her salt will tell you a few things worth knowing in this area:

- we cannot force anyone to DO anything (in the long term)
- we can only create the environment where they WANT to do it, because they SEE a benefit in doing it

In a nutshell, how we SEE the world/situation/organisation/role/issue, dictates what we DO about it. (And what we 'DO' has consequences dictated by the circumstances, which usually reinforces the way we SEE the world). (See diagram)

The issue therefore was (and usually is in 99% of cases), that those who were trying to influence my views on customer service and enable me to do it better, were focusing on the 'DO' part of the equation. So until I (or you, or anyone else) 'SEES' the situation differently, we are not going to do anything different. There's no point in teaching the horse HOW to drink water if it's not thirsty/can't get to the water.

The other problem is that, when we 'DO' something, the results we 'GET' will generally reinforce the way we 'SAW' the issue in the first place. This is called a 'self fulfilling prophecy'. So, for example: if I am a telephone operative in an organisation and I have been trained and asked to smile on every phone call, I'm only going to 'DO' this if I 'SEE' something to smile about.

If I am well paid, well treated, rewarded for giving great service and have the necessary tools and systems to do my job properly, then I'll probably do this. If I think my boss is a bozo, the management are embezzlers and the systems are junk, even if I'm well rewarded, I'm unlikely to be a top smiler.

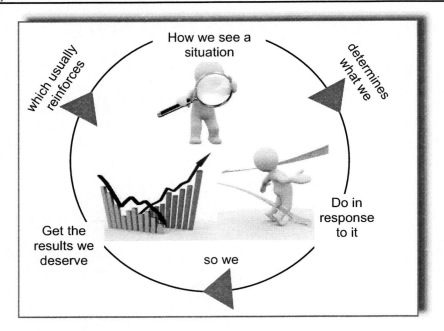

So we have to pay some serious attention to the 'SEE' side of the issue, before we go stampeding towards the 'DO' bit. Unfortunately many managers and leaders miss this out, assuming that everyone has the same motivation (even if they have a miserable role, in a dank office and are paid in peanuts) and should just get on with it or get out of it.

Conversely if their people don't have this motivation, they often assume one of the following things:

- They're lazy
- They're unmotivated
- They're sloppy
- They're unorganised
- They're idiots

Not a very positive situation. Yet, so often, when I do seminars and talks and ask the question 'why isn't it common practice?' - these are the responses I always get.

I also get the following answers:

- Don't have time (a very common response)
- Don't know how to do it
- Don't know what's important
- Stopped by systems/processes/measures
- Wrong person in the wrong job, and the universal chestnut
- Poor communication.

In some rare cases, they might just be right, but let's just look at each of these with regards 'SEE' and 'DO'.

Response	What it really means
They're idiots	They don't SEE it as important or else they'd be doing it.
Don't have time	Don't SEE it as important enough, otherwise they'd be prioritising better.
Don't know what's important	Don't SEE it consistently.
Stopped by systems/processes/measures	If we SAW it as important, all these systems, processes and measures would be aligned to delivering excellent customer service.
Wrong person in the wrong job	This does happen, and the kindest thing for all parties is to find them a job they are good at ASAP. But very often this is yet again a 'SEE' issue: they aren't giving the service because they don't SEE why it's necessary (for whatever reason).
Poor Communication	We don't SEE things clearly or in the same way, because we haven't taken the time to communicate properly. So things get DONE wrong.

Here's an example of this working in practice:

A washer upper in a restaurant was demotivated and disillusioned. She worked in a small dank room, where it was hot and stuffy and had to deal with dirty plates, mixed with napkins and waste for ten hours a day. Her back hurt and although she felt well paid (and was given a fair share of the tips), she just didn't feel the desire or the need to do the job excellently.

Consequently, sometimes plates weren't ready in time, or were put in the wrong place or the wrong order. Cutlery wasn't well polished and sometimes even had food specks on it. Everyone was unhappy! She was, the kitchen staff were and the customers were!

Her manager repeatedly asked her to DO things better and this would result in her improving for a while, but the old issues would simply resurface again and results deteriorated.

The manager asked a friend what he could do about it. He said: "I'm going to have to get rid of her, but I can't find anyone else". The friend advised him to SEE the issue differently and to help her SEE the issue differently.

So the manager tried again. This time he approached the situation less like a bull in a china shop. He took time to praise her when things were put away properly or the cutlery shined particularly well. He made a point of taking her coffee and donuts. He asked her what he could do to make her job easier and some small, inexpensive but very worthwhile improvements were made.

He sought advice on back problems, taught her how to stand so that her back would ache less and encouraged her to stretch and take breaks. He bought her out at quieter times to meet and interact with the customers - many of them told her how nice it was to have sparkling clean plates and cutlery.

When all this was done, he encouraged her to speak with the other members of staff, to ask them how she could help them better and in turn, how they could help her better. And so in doing all of this, huge operational improvements (that cost nothing) were put into place.

When he had finally built up her trust and commitment, he shared his previous feelings - in full. She was shocked to hear how low she had become and what a huge impact her performance had made on the business. She suggested other ways that improvements could be made, including how she could multi-task and cross skill to make processes more efficient. She became committed and excellent.

All because:

One person changed the way he SAW the problem
And one person changed the way she SAW her role

(and, of course, the changes that were implemented were all common sense).

So, in order to answer the question why isn't it common practice? It seems we have to work at a different level. We have to 'SEE' right first, before we address the 'DO'. If we 'GET' all this right, then we'll 'GET' the right result.

Here's a great story that makes this point better than I ever could:

> The boards of two fiercely competitive companies decided to organise a rowing match, to challenge each other's organisational and sporting abilities. The first company (let's call it company 'X') was ruthless and autocratic with zero staff empowerment. The second company (company 'Y') had a culture of developing people, devolved responsibility and decision-making.
>
> Race day arrived. Company Y's boat appeared from the boat-house first, with its crew - eight rowers and a helmsman (the Cox). Next followed company X's boat and its crew - eight helmsmen and a single rower. Not surprisingly, company Y's boat won an easy victory.
>
> The next day company X's board of directors held an inquest with the crew, to review what had been learned from the embarrassing defeat, which might be of benefit to the organisation as a whole and any future re-match.
>
> After a long and wearing meeting the company X's board finally came to their decision. They concluded that the rower should be replaced immediately, because clearly he had not listened well enough to the instructions he'd been given.

How often does this happen in organisations today?

The following chapters are arranged to focus on 'SEE' first, then 'DO' and then how to measure the 'GET' (for we have no control over the 'GET', it is simply a natural consequence of the 'DO').

Here's an outline of the rest of the book, relating it to this concept:

SECTION TWO	
What's the answer?	How can we SEE this differently?
Customer focused Mission.	How we SEE the role of our whole organisation.
Be 'great'.	Once we SEE things differently, how do we DO things really well?
SECTION THREE	
Tools and tips.	SEE things differently. DO things differently.
How to measure 'greatness'.	How does our customer SEE us? How do we measure what we DO so we can identify issues
Conclusion.	Do we SEE this strongly enough to DO what it takes to change?
Action planning.	What can we DO differently now we SEE the issue and the opportunity differently?

In order to address this properly, therefore, we need to look at a simple model of how all organisations work - big and small - and then see where the gaps and issues often occur.

The 'organisational effectiveness' model

This is a model used extensively by the Franklin Covey organisation (www.franklincovey.com) and is a simple (but powerful) diagram, showing the basic cycle that makes all organisations work.

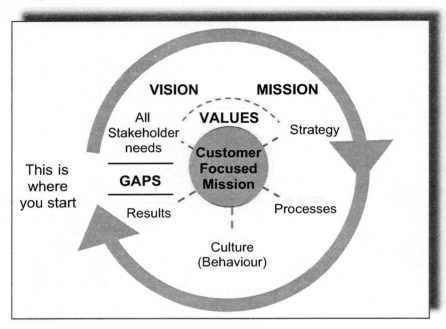

Stakeholders:

Any organisation has stakeholders. The word 'stakeholder' means a person or group that has an investment, share, or interest in something, as a business or industry.

So this can be (in no particular order):

- Shareholders
- Partners
- Owners
- Employees
- Customers
- Suppliers
- The community
- Everyone

These stakeholders have a 'Vision' (see Appendix 1), and this 'Vision' will inspire a 'Mission'.

Mission: (see Appendix 1)

Every organisation has a 'Mission' (whether they know it or not!). A 'Mission', is defined as:

- An assigned or self-imposed duty or task, calling, vocation.
- A sending or being sent for some duty or purpose.

In other words, this is 'what we do' (the 'Vision' provides the 'why' often called the 'gap in the market'). The 'Mission' is the root of everything that happens within an organisation, it is the driver of activity and the fulcrum around which decisions are made. So the Mission is quite important, but VERY often abused or ignored (we'll come to that later).

In an ideal situation, the Mission will be:

- Clear
- Unambiguous
- Focused on ALL stakeholder needs
- Supported by all personnel
- Used as the fount of all strategy and procedures, and
- Adhered to rigidly by all.

And it will, therefore, produce the:

Strategy

A strategy will be consistent with the 'Mission', but will adapt to conditions and opportunity. In fact, it will be continually growing and evolving with the growth and evolution of the organisation and the change in environment. (Note: this process of change and evolution is becoming faster and faster - so a well thought out 'Mission' is essential).

I like this definition of strategy, as it says it all:

A plan, method, or series of manoeuvres or stratagems for obtaining a specific goal or result: a strategy for getting ahead in the world.

We all know how important strategy is. It needs to be VERY clear from the top down, consistent with the 'Mission' and empowering further strategy throughout an organisation in support of it.

Strategy will deliver:

Processes

We all think we know what processes are, but what does the word actually mean?

- A systematic series of actions directed to some end.

The key words here are:

- systematic: i.e. driven by a system (not by the will of God)
- actions: things that happen
- directed to some end: in line with the 'Mission' and strategy

So, with all these wonderful processes, we'll have wonderful:

Behaviour

What people actually do.

There's a plethora of different interpretations of 'behaviour', but it's basically as stated above. Of course, if the stakeholders are acting functionally, the 'Mission', strategy and processes are clear and aligned, then the behaviour will generally be excellent.

In this scenario, if it isn't, there's a behavioural issue to address (which can be tricky), but as all the other aspects are aligned and functioning properly, at least we will know where to address the action. (And this is why in 95% of cases, the judgements of why great service doesn't happen are so often mistaken. We can't effectively make this judgement until all of the above are aligned and revolving around a clear and empowering CFM - a rare situation indeed).

Of course, behaviour will always give us results, exactly aligned to stakeholders needs - all of the time!

They aren't?

Why not?

That is the question we try to answer in this chapter.

So what actually happens in reality? The crux of the issue is this. The above scenario shows how it can work, but, in reality it's not quite as simple, clear and well organised as this. Many organisations have grown and prospered without this all being clear. Many have come out of mergers, many have been lucky (and many more have disappeared), but research shows that those that prosper in the long term, are those that have got this right.

So let's examine the reality of 'organisational effectiveness' from a customer service perspective. But before we get into the detail, here are some questions for you to consider honestly from your organisation's point of view:

- When there are behavioural problems, are ALL aspects of the diagram considered or just the behaviour?
- Do ALL the stakeholders have the same aspirations or is there a conflict?
- When times are hard, what changes?
- When customer service is considered, where on the diagram is it focused?
- In fact, where is 95% of all training and development focused?
- When push comes to shove which areas get pushed aside to get the bottom line figures?

With regards to the customer's point of view, let's start at the very beginning - a very good place to start!

Stakeholders:

The questions we need to address (and some proposed answers) are:

Are all the stakeholders treated with equal importance?	Very rarely.
Which stakeholder's needs generally push the others' out of the way when 'times are hard'?	You've guessed it: the owners / shareholders and everyone else becomes fed up and disillusioned (and surprisingly, don't give great service, no matter how hard they are pushed or cajoled or 'incentivised').
What happens when certain stakeholders' needs are repressed or ignored?	Disaster: • Owners needs ignored: organisation doesn't survive. • Employees' needs ignored: organisation struggles to deliver what it says it will and customer service is not good! • Suppliers needs ignored: supply difficulties make it hard to deliver great service. • Customer needs ignored: organisation dies when a competitor comes along. • Customer doesn't feedback issues because there's no goodwill - they just go elsewhere. • Community needs ignored: organisation consistently struggles to keep people and expand. • Getting any of these wrong is like having a cancer eating away at your organisation.
Why did the stakeholders become stakeholders, and what effect will this have?	This is critical: If the organisation is not clearly aligned around 'worthwhile' 'Mission / Vision / Values' (i.e. pointing North), then stakeholders can ONLY consider their own needs when being a stakeholder. If the alignment is clear and worthwhile, then the organisation will attract like-minded stakeholders (e.g. The Co-Op bank in the UK), who will work tirelessly to achieve the aims. If not, the only reward is MONEY (and this will bleed you dry). This is ably demonstrated by the huge influence that major shareholders have on Plc's in the UK. Simply put, they are often only interested in short term return, not in long term growth. Unless they are VERY carefully managed, eventually their parasitic attitude will kill the host. You have been warned.

So there are a lot of pitfalls that our poor unfortunate stakeholders can cause for our organisation, resulting in disillusionment, dysfunctional behaviour and poor customer service.

The solution:

- Make sure the 'Vision', 'Mission', and 'values' are clear, worthwhile and aligned.
- Recruit stakeholders around this.
- If they don't 'buy in' they don't 'get in'.
- Get rid of the stakeholders who aren't aligned.

Then you'll be sailing downwind.

In effect, it's a bit upside down. The 'Mission' has to be clear before the stakeholders can be recruited, because if not, they'll be aligned around values that are misaligned at best, and contradictory at worst.

This is easier to do for a startup organisation, but in reality, most people and organisations do not have this luxury.

So the process has to be:

- Get the 'Mission' clear,
- then ensure GENUINE stakeholder buy-in,
- then deal with the strategy, processes, and behaviour.

But the stakeholders hold all the sway to this and from a customer service perspective, they have to believe (and be prepared to put their money where their mouth is) that:

**We are in business to deliver a service
that is so good people are prepared to pay for it**

i.e.

**Service first
profits second
always**

and unless ALL your stakeholders definitely agree and are prepared to see this through and actually make it work (rather than just a cheesy slogan), then you'll NEVER deliver great customer service consistently and excellently.

And the amazing thing is, most stakeholders won't thank you for telling them this. We live in a dysfunctional world, and this is going against the grain.

Let me repeat this.

Either: all stakeholders believe and do this or you can't deliver great service consistently and excellently

It's very simple and very true - just ask any employee, supplier or community whose needs have not been addressed by the organisation.

Mission (for more details please see Appendix 1)

Let's say we do actually have a fantastic bunch of functional aligned stakeholders. Their 'Vision' will determine the Mission. (I love talking about Mission statements, because people start to twitch uncomfortably on their seats, and I have a real challenge).

The word 'Mission' must be one of the most abused of the 20th century. People's eyes glaze over because they've heard and seen all the Mission statements you could think possible. And they all mean the same thing. Naff all.

Well, actually it's not all bad - they do actually serve a purpose. They really get under employees' (and customers') skin, annoy them and make them start looking around for alternative places to work or do business.

Here are some great ones that will really annoy you (with the name of the organisation omitted for obvious reasons):

"To be the pre-eminent .... Company in the US." (What does this mean?)
"To be the best ... in the Greater London area." (How do you measure this?)
"To generate long term shareholder return." (What about the other stakeholders?)
"To deliver world class ...."

And how about the ones that go on forever and no one can remember them - what's the point?

And the classic cheesy ones:

"We value the customer."
"Your success is our success."
"Simply the best."

Here are some gobbledygook classics:

"Our Mission is to quickly negotiate corporate sources, so that we may endeavour to competently restore value-added solutions to meet our customer's needs."

"We continually revolutionize business data to allow us to quickly integrate unique solutions to stay competitive in tomorrow's world."

"It's our responsibility to globally build virtual services so that we may endeavour to completely promote high-payoff paradigms to exceed customer expectations."

These three came straight from the 'Dilbert Mission Statement Generator' but you see their similitudes all around you. Some old schoolers even post them on their websites.

Not that all Mission statements are dumb and pointless, but the good and meaningful ones are so hard to find. Here are some very good ones (that have enabled the organisation to build success):

3M: *"To solve unsolved problems innovatively."*

Merck: *"To preserve and improve human life."*

Wal-Mart: *"To give ordinary folk the chance to buy the same thing as rich people."*

Walt Disney: *"To make people happy."*

Tesco: *"Every little helps."*

These are the 'one-liners' that actually mean something to each and every one of the employees within the organisation. Each is supported by a set of values that set the performance standards and direct the implementation of the Mission, but each is worthwhile common sense and gives each and every employee clear and positive guidance, in every thing they do every day - consistently and excellently.

For example, Merck, a company that produces pharmaceutical products and provides insurance for pharmacy benefits, publicly states the following values.

- Corporate social responsibility.
- Unequivocal excellence in all aspects of the company.
- Science-based innovation.
- Honesty and integrity.
- Profit, but profit from work that benefits humanity.

And Walt Disney, an entertainment business states their values as follows.

- No cynicism.
- Nurturing and promulgation of "wholesome American values".
- Creativity, dreams and imagination.
- Fanatical attention to consistency and detail.
- Preservation and control of the Disney "magic".

So these all work well, but most Mission statements don't. Guy Kawasaki sums it up in his book, 'The Art of the Start':

> "The fundamental shortcoming of most Mission statements is that everyone expects them to be highfaluting and all-encompassing. The result is a long, boring, commonplace and pointless joke. [...] Companies are all writing the same mediocre things."

Exactly!

The one-liners work well, as they are a simple statement based on the REALITY of the customer's needs for everyone to identify with and remember. They also give the feeling of achievability.

A company a friend of mine once worked for, came up with a new Mission statement. Trying to remember it word perfect was a nightmare - a bit like a policeman reading someone their rights. The Director would often, when meeting staff, ask them to quote the statement. If you got it right, he was as pleased as punch. Funny though, he never asked how things were going and if there was anything they thought he could do to improve things.

This is called:

Chasing Butterflies whilst the Elephants are Escaping.

So, from a customer service perspective, what really happens is this (and associated issues caused).

The owners set the 'Mission' around their needs.	No one buys into it, and EVERYONE is fed up and disillusioned, because not only do the other stakeholders become demotivated and disillusioned, but also the owners don't get what they want, and spend all their time trying to manage the 'do'. Lose / Lose
The 'Mission' is set properly, but hard times come along and strategy is implemented that is the antithesis of it.	The true test of any system is when times are tough and all the other stakeholders remember this forever. Remember: actions speak louder than words.
The 'Mission' keeps changing.	Chaos and pointlessness.
The 'Mission' is set properly, but the leaders don't stick to it.	Resentment and bitterness on all levels, and disastrous levels of service. Actions speak louder than words.
The 'Mission' is set properly, but the strategy and processes haven't been designed around achieving it.	Disillusionment, chaos and conflict. People will try to do their best usually, but this will really test them.
The 'Mission' is set properly, but the behaviour doesn't reflect it, and no one sorts it out.	More resentment and very low levels of commitment.
There is no clear Mission.	Variable levels of service at best. Often accompanied with confusion and frustration at all levels.

If you think this is all a bit confusing, or a bit too true to life, here's a real example:

Enron's Mission statement noted that the company prided itself on four key values: respect, integrity, communication and excellence. Among other things, all business dealings at Enron were supposed to be 'open and fair'. As Enron's story unfolded in Congress, it was obvious the former seventh-largest U.S. Company wasn't living up to its own Mission statement.

So now the questions for you and your organisation are:

- Is your 'Mission' clear, functional, worthwhile, empowering and aligned with the 'Vision'?
- Have you even thought about it?
- Do you and your people believe it and live it - obsessively?
- Do your personal 'Mission' and 'values' link to it?
- Do your 'values' reflect the 'Mission'?
- Do your strategies and processes flow from it?
- Is behaviour measured around it?

Because, if not, here's another root of customer dissatisfaction.

So let's take this a step further towards customer service excellence. My view is simple (and Blindly Obvious Common Sense). As well as being functional, worthwhile, empowering and aligned, your 'Mission' must be:

Customer focused

What this means is that, if you're a service organisation (and EVERYONE is), you MUST base your 'Mission' around your customers needs, and not yours.

If you focus your 'Mission' on your customer needs and get it right you'll exceed your own needs. If you don't, you won't.

We'll talk more about this in later chapters.

Strategy

Organisations spend huge amounts of time deliberating over, changing and communicating strategy and the usual response is:

"Oh, that's flavour of the month at the moment is it?"

And everyone just carries on doing what they've always done (and getting what they've always got).

When hard times appear, Organisations have enormous reorganisations and restructures (and downsizing), but if the root of all this (the 'Mission') isn't right, it will make precious little difference (apart from changing a few job titles and some overheads).

But if the root is right and is Customer Focused, then all of this becomes unnecessary. All strategy will naturally flow from the 'Mission', all departments will be able to use central strategy to create local strategy, because they have the 'Mission' to guide them. When times are hard, the 'Mission' will show them what to do. Downsizing may be necessary, but all will understand why and will generally be supportive. A great 'Mission' makes it easy.

So what can go wrong with strategy? Some ideas:

Strategy not aligned with 'Mission'.	Disillusionment and confusion. Departments will often be working against each other in effect.
Strategy not Customer Focused.	People constantly having to tell the customer that 'it's not our policy to do that' and the customer consequently getting fed up and looking elsewhere for satisfaction.
Strategy aligned with Mission but people don't know what the 'Mission' is.	Could be OK, but will be pot luck.
Strategy constantly changing.	Confusion and lack of ownership / "I only work here."

Setting, explaining and sticking to Strategy is easy when the 'Mission' is clear - and impossible when it's not.

In order to deliver excellent customer service, these two have to be clearly aligned and focused on customer needs.

There's little else to say.

Processes

I so often hear complaints about (and personally experience) processes that aren't aligned around customer needs and, by now I expect you have got the picture!

All processes need to be aligned with strategy (which in turn needs to be aligned with 'Mission' etc). In other words there needs to be 'clear line of sight' between all processes and the 'Mission'.

But this rarely happens. We've all experienced:

- Service companies that give great offers to new customers that aren't available to existing ones.
- Banks that drop interest rates on savings accounts after you've been with them for a while.
- Over zealous credit controllers who treat you with contempt for a first offence.
- Trains that are late but no one bothers to tell you.
- Endless waits on phone answering systems.
- Customer service departments you can't speak to.
- Customer service departments that don't have authority to make a decision.
- Websites that make it next to impossible to have a great experience.

This last point poses an interesting conundrum. Some websites, despite being completely automised, provide a great customer experience. So, if done well, a website can make the customer experience systematically excellent. But we can't do all our business over the web.

Most of us will have to deal face to face and on the telephone at some point. Very often this is where the real issues lays. We all know what it's like dealing with an Internet organisation that is great 'on line', but when you have to deal with a person, the experience suddenly becomes a nightmare.

Here's a good example from the UK in 2007.

"It is a year since Carphone Warehouse shook up the market with its 'free' broadband offer, but many consumers are still waiting to be connected, while others continue to be plagued by poor service.

Carphone launched its cut-price Talk-Talk service this time last year, but was swamped by orders, resulting in some customers having to wait months to be connected. Many have left and others are having to put up with poor service".

So this is clearly an area that may seem easy, but in reality can be somewhat tricky. We need to ask ourselves:

- Where are issues likely to arise?
- How will we deal with them?
- Is everyone who deals with them empowered to make the right decisions at that moment in time?
- How easy do we make it for the customer to resolve issues?
- And how do we know what is really happening before it becomes a problem?

Because even if the processes are aligned with the strategy, 'Mission' and stakeholder needs (so that we have a clear 'line of sight' between stakeholder needs and the processes (based on a Customer Focused Mission), it can still all go pear shaped at the last hurdle:

Behaviour

Remember the principle:

No one is trying to do a bad job
(and in fact, everyone is trying to do their best)

So, if we identify poor customer service behaviour, we need to SEE why it has happened before we attempt to DO something about it.

Here are some ideas as to why it could be happening.

The employee doesn't want to do a good job. SEE	• Unclear Mission
The employee is trying to do a good job but failing. SEE or DO	• Dysfunctional Mission
	• Dysfunctional behaviour further up
The employee doesn't enjoy the role. SEE	• Over demanding stakeholders
	• Misaligned strategy
The employee doesn't know what to DO	• Misaligned processes
The employee feels disillusioned. SEE	• Lack of training
	• Unclear job role
The employee feels let down. SEE	• Having a bad day
The employee is poorly treated. SEE	• Or they might just be the wrong person in the wrong job
The employee is rewarded for dysfunctional behaviour by a misaligned process. SEE	

So, just working at the DO level (where 95% of customer service activity is focused) will only resolve about 20% of issues.

The 80/20 rule strikes again.

Spend at least 20% of your total efforts at the SEE level, and the return will be huge and lasting.

To sum up this part of the chapter:

- Stakeholder needs, Mission, Strategy, Processes and Behaviour rewards need to be obsessively and consistently aligned around a customer focus.
- When this is done, employees will be empowered and motivated to deliver great service and resolve issues.
- When this isn't done, the best you can hope for is benign confusion at all levels.

So, work spent getting this right, is time well spent. Please also read Appendix 1 with this chapter, as there have been plenty of well meaning attempts throughout history to resolve these issues, but so often, they have tried to effect a 'quick fix'. This won't work. If people are not involved with the process from Step 1, they won't be committed to it.

It takes time, it takes patience, and it takes obsessive commitment.

Unfortunately these are also qualities that are often in short supply.

Here's a simple exercise you can complete, or ask others to complete or share with you, to help you address issues in this area.

Who are the stakeholders?

Are their needs aligned to the delivery of customer delight?

What about when the going gets tough?

What is the Mission / Vision?

Is it aligned to the delivery of customer delight?

Does everyone know this?

What about when the going gets tough?

What about the strategies and processes?

Aligned to the delivery of customer delight?

Not aligned to the delivery of customer delight?

Where are the internal conflicts?

What gets in the way?

What about behaviours?

Mine

Others

Is it aligned to the delivery of customer delight?

What about when the going gets tough?

ACTIONS	
In my circle of influence	Who do I need to tell?
In my circle of influence	Who do I need to speak to?

What other issues can there be?

I expect that if you made a list of other issues, it would be fairly long, so here are some key ones. My belief is that if you get these right, most of the others will take care of themselves. But beware, a lot of this is very unpopular, especially with Accountants and Finance Directors.

The upside down triangle

When I go into organisations I always ask them to show me a copy of their organisation's chart, showing people's role and positions.   I am still waiting for the first one to show me one that's focused on delivering great service to customers. They always show me something looking like this:

So what's wrong with this? Nothing if it's all about ego and telling people what to do. (Which is called 'The Industrial Age mindset').

In fact this type of structure works well for setting Mission and strategy, but when it comes to processes and behaviour, this is a disaster.

Here are some thought provoking questions for you to consider:

- Who's the most important person on this chart?
- Where is the customer?
- What level of importance does the customer hold?
- At what level are the main customer facing personnel and are they likely to be listened to?
- Who knows best: top or bottom?
- In a situation of conflict, who would win: the one above or the one below?

In a truly Customer Focused organisation, might this work better the other way up?

Remember pictures speak much louder than words. Go for something that looks a bit more like this:

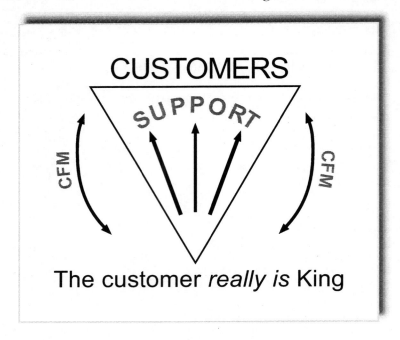

500-year old accounting policies

A simple, but hugely influential point. Current standard accounting practices were invented about 500 years ago. They regard machinery and buildings as 'investments' and people and development as 'overheads'. What type of behaviour is this likely to engender? Especially when times get hard.

Perhaps some new thinking and rules are needed for the 21st century. Just try and SEE people as 'investments' and watch your behaviour and processes change.

The Industrial Age mentality

This links to the above two points and was explored in detail earlier (remember the 'rowing match' story?). Basically, this is a very prevalent mindset in the West and the reason many of our manufacturing businesses have gone elsewhere (soon to be followed by the much hyped service industries, as soon as the Eastern organisations truly get their act together).

There was a quote from a Japanese industrialist about 15 years ago which went a bit like this (the accuracy is not as important as the point).

> *"We will always win, because you believe the person who knows how to do the job is the person in the boardroom whereas, we believe it's the person doing the job itself. You are wrong and we are right and there's nothing you can do about it".*

How true! But there is something we can all do about it.

It's never too late to change and the people doing the jobs are crying out for this change. People want to be valued in their jobs more than anything else and the organisations that do this will blow the competition away.

Here's a quote from the Times in the UK in 2008:

> "The three winners of this year's 'Best Companies to Work For' competitions were announced last week at a glittering awards ceremony in London. Although the winners range in size from 123 to 11,872 employees, they are three of a kind – employers who put their workforce first and who, in return, get levels of commitment and engagement that others can only dream of."

The devil is in the detail

This is often called 'Moments of Truth'. This was a phrase coined by Jan Carlzon, CEO of SAS, on how he used this concept to turn around the Scandinavian airline and enabled it to become a synonym for excellent service throughout the customer experience. It's a simple concept, but very hard to achieve: basically it's this:

- Every interaction a customer has with your organisation is a 'moment of truth', i.e. true for them, the customer.`
- So the only way to make sure you deliver great customer service consistently, is to examine every "Moment Of Truth" from the customer's point of view, analyse every outcome and ensure there is a Customer Focused system in place to deal with each and every one.
- Alongside making sure all your people have the information, support, systems, processes, and motivation to solve every problem at the moment it happens: the moment of truth. This is called empowerment.
- This empowers everyone at all levels to make a <u>decision</u> at that moment. If they can't do this, then the moment is lost and the customer gets poor service.

Hard to do, but worth it.

To take this a bit further, and using the airline business as an analogy, the customer expects to:

- Get to the destination on time, fed, and in one piece.
- Get his or her baggage there as well.

What will 'blow him or her away' is:

- Being treated like a valuable person, rather than just a ticket.

This is achieved by thinking through all processes in great detail (by the people who are actually doing the job) and designing the processes around achieving this goal.

So, for example:

- Making check in easy.
- Offering services that <u>really</u> make the customer's life easier.
- Knowing preferences.
- Considering in-flight details that others overlook.
- Etc.

So the SYSTEMS need to consider every avenue and need to be supported by people with the right ATTITUDE. Every member of staff must take responsibility and inwardly imagine it is their business, not pass the buck and think, "not my problem, I just work here".

This is a true story that a friend witnessed in a Hotel where he was the Area Manager.

I had been attending a meeting the previous evening and stayed over, which gave me an opportunity to experience the level of hospitality. At breakfast an elderly couple were sat on the next table to mine. The gentleman ordered smoked haddock. When the waitress entered the restaurant the smell was unbelievable. My immediate thought was, "if he takes one mouthful he's dead".

The gentleman's wife told him that she thought the fish was off, but he did not want to make a fuss. Before I could dive in doing a 'Fawlty Towers' impression, the wife called over the waitress, told her she was not happy and asked if her husband could order something else.

The waitress took away the plate and as she entered the kitchen, we all heard her shout,

"You were right Chef, it is off."

Here's a simple spreadsheet to help you look at this and improve your Moments of Truth on an ongoing basis.

Once you've got your 'Mission' and strategy sorted, this is one of the processes you can use to make it happen!

Exercise: Moments of Truth:

1. Identify the Moments of Truth (you may need to keep asking your customers).
2. Look at what systems are needed to produce excellence (there may well be a few).
3. Identify and set up, measures to ensure they get delivered ongoing.

What?	System?	Measures in Place	Measures Needed

ACTIONS	
In my circle of influence	**Who do I need to tell?**
In my circle of influence	**Who do I need to speak to?**

Don't worry, Rome wasn't built in a day. It won't and can't happen overnight, but if all are pulling in the same direction, it's only a matter of time. And even more good news - the measurement process shown later in this book will enable you to ensure this is a continually evolving and improving process.

Of course the most important part of any moment of truth is the commitment to continue it.

- In The TGI Friday Restaurants, the serving staff always used to squat down when taking your order and put balloons on the back of children's chairs. Do they still do that?

- Do the AA patrols still salute their customers?

Because, no matter what the intention of the organisation, the 'truth' is how this is perceived by the customer, each and every day in every little interaction.

As you experience customer service every day as a customer yourself, give some thought to those companies that offer as a point of difference, that little bit extra, that extra "touch" and then ask yourself, "why do they do that?".

Moment Of Truths are not a gimmick. Attention to them is what sets your company apart from the others and makes you great. You'll notice the more attention you pay to them, the more empowered your people will become to deal with them and service and motivation levels will begin to soar.

To finish this section off, here are some quotes from Mr. Carlzon, referred to earlier:

"We have 50,000 Moments of Truth every day", referring to every time an employee of the company came into contact with a customer.

"An individual without information can't take responsibility. An individual with information can't help but take responsibility."

"Mistakes can usually be corrected later; the time that is lost in not making a decision can never be retrieved.".

"The right to make mistakes is not equivalent to the right to be incompetent, especially not as a manager."

Trust and hidden agendas

Very simply, trust is the oil that lubricates everything else.

Low trust is a tax on a business and high trust is a dividend. The only way to build trust is to do trustworthy things. For example, making sure the Mission, strategy and processes are joined up and Customer Focused, but most importantly:

- sticking to them no matter what
- leading by example
- treating everyone with courtesy
- being firm and consistent
- having clear pricing and boundaries
- treating customers new and old the same, and incredibly
- doing what you say you will do

This one simple point is one upon which so many individuals and organisations flounder. So much goodwill and good action is wasted through lack of execution. There's plenty that can be done to address this and we'll look at this in the third section of this book. One 'trust blunder' can undo months or even years of high trust activity and even if all the Mission, strategy and processes are Customer Focused, if management don't practice it personally, it will immediately go out of the window.

For further information on trust, it's well worth reading 'The Speed of Trust' by Stephen M R Covey.

For now, please just remember this.

**In essence, all a customer wants is to TRUST you
sort out their problem
and to make their life better!**

If you build trust with a customer, you make his or her life better - which is what we all want. If you make my life better as a customer, I'm going to be much less interested in your price, and the other trivial details.

That's why Ronseal get their advertising so right, when they say:

'It does exactly what it says on the tin.'

This has added greatness 'built in', because it implies that none of the other products from other companies do what they say 'on the tin'!

Here's another example of someone who was trying to get their satellite dish fitted.

> Last week a local agent fitted my new dish. All was well until after a few days, when I suddenly could not get a signal. The people that fitted it are all of one mile away from where I live. I rang them on the Friday night, the partner answered,
>
> "Andy is not in at the moment, I'll talk to him when he gets in and we will be in touch tomorrow morning."
>
> Saturday morning came - no phone call.
>
> I rang them and get Andy. He had no clue what I was talking about and so I told him my issue.

"It should not do that", he said helpfully.

Well there's a bloody surprise! I was beginning to think it was all my problem and I was being a nuisance. He said he'd be in touch Monday.

Monday morning came - no call. I rang them again and get Andy's partner, who said,

"Oh Hi, I was just looking up your number". After much teeth sucking, she said she'd pop round and have a look after 5.00 pm that night.

In my situation what trust or faith should I have in this company?

What is blindingly obvious common sense, is that on Friday night, someone should have come straight out. They are a local company recently set up and are one mile away. At the very least they could have come out on Saturday.

What gets measured gets done

This is critical. The Olympic Champion English rower, Steve Redgrave, tells the story of how the team studied and estimated the 'winning time' for each Olympic race and then set their training around achieving this time over the four years available. The key thing was that they measured progress towards one winning time on a weekly and even daily, basis.

All self improvement gurus will tell you that, in order to achieve what you want, you need to set SMART goals.

Imagine the shock at a shareholders' meeting if the FD stood up and announced that, although they didn't have any figures, he or she was pretty sure they were 'doing OK' because they'd paid most of their bills and the Bank Manager hadn't phoned to complain.

Yet this is how 99% of organisations measure the most critical factor determining the success of their business: customer service!

Organisations tend to be great at measuring 'lag' measures (e.g. profit and loss), and one of the great things about money is that it's easy to measure (which is in reality why it's so powerful). But these same organisations tend to look at me blankly and with pity, when I suggest they start measuring 'lead' measures.

A 'lead' measure is a measure that predicts future success. These types of measure are hard to find and you have to be obsessive about them. But, they are hugely powerful, because if you get them right, they will enable you to predict problems and opportunities and deal with them way before it's too late.

Why do people not use them? There are a number of reasons:

1. People don't know about them. (Well now you do!)
2. Because they can't be proven, they're an act of faith: You have to have faith that, if you set and measure these things, then you will have success in the longer term.
3. They never come and find you: You have to go and look for them and everyone is just so busy aren't they?
4. You have to be obsessive and consistent about them, otherwise they won't get done.

This is far too ethereal in our rush for short term cash.

That's why it works.

So, if you can find a realistic and proven, measure that will tell you scientifically how you're doing against your 'Mission' (and give you all the information you need to address the issues), that would be powerful would it not?

This is the fourth major question that this book addresses and in effect, the key to everything else.

Because, what gets measured gets done.

Despite us thinking how liberated we are as people, we basically have only two reasons to do anything;

1. to escape pain (by far the biggest motivator): 'away from motivation'
2. to pursue pleasure : 'towards motivation'

A realistic and compelling measure ticks both these boxes.

So there we have it: the full gambit of 'what gets in the way'.

Here's a summary.

What gets in the way?	What can we do about it?
Misaligned stakeholder needs, Mission, strategy and processes.	Align all these around a true customer focus, called a 'Customer Focused Mission'.
Misaligned behaviour.	SEE what the issue really is before doing anything.
500 year old accounting policies.	Re-invent the way you account for your organisation and ensure all the stakeholders are bought into this.
The Industrial Age mindset.	Re-engineer the Mission, strategy and processes around the 'knowledge age' mentality. Get rid of industrial age stakeholders and behaviours.
Moments of Truth not addressed.	Constant obsessive and consistent attention via a system of analysis and review, on the details from the customers' point of view and the guts to change things before they become an issue.
Lack of trust.	Build trust in every interaction and lead by example at all levels.
No realistic measure.	Put in a realistic measure incentivise and discipline around it - this should be more important than the P&L. What gets measured gets done.

"That's all very well, but what can I do if I'm not the MD?"

Of course it's easier to change things when you're MD (and sometimes it isn't - you should see some of the stakeholders they have to deal with!). The point is:

Do the best you can with whatever you have.
Create your own sphere of excellence in your own circle of influence.

Because your only other option is to give up and go home. And that's not an option.

I leave you with a quote from Anne Frank (who had more reason than most for despair).

"How wonderful it is that nobody need wait a single moment before starting to improve the world."

SECTION TWO

Chapter One: What's the answer?

I believe that the only way things will get done, is to keep them simple and easy to remember.

So, for great customer service, there are four simple steps to take:

1. Create a Customer Focused Mission.
2. Understand and act around the customer's REAL needs.
3. Deliver consistently and go the extra inch.
4. Measure consistently and obsessively.

What is the thinking behind this?

The Mission is the root of all activity. If the Mission is Customer Focused (with passion and integrity), then the roots of the organisation will be sound and will enable it to grow and thrive (and hopefully survive a drought). By making it Customer Focused, you're giving out two clear messages.

- To customers: we're here for you and the only way we'll thrive is if we do what's right for you.
- To other stakeholders: this is what we do - if you like it, come and be part of it, if you don't, please don't.

There's a lot of information in Appendix 1 about 'Mission', 'Vision' and 'values', so please refer to this.

When the Mission is clear, we have a clear direction and purpose. Then we can take stock and strive to understand and act around the customer's real needs. Most organisations do the opposite. They look for the 'gap in the market' and then try and fill it. The result is:

- Constantly changing priorities.
- Disengaged stakeholders.
- Unclear priorities.

It will work for a time. However, the time will come when the 'gap' closes or, more likely, someone else enters the market who does have a Customer Focused Mission and they'll take the market overnight. It happens all the time.

For example, Google were not the first search engine on the market by any means. Google began in January 1996, as a research project by Larry Page, who was soon joined by Sergey Brin. They hypothesised that a search engine that analysed the relationships between websites would produce better ranking of results than existing techniques, which ranked results according to the number of times the search term appeared on a page.

Convinced that the pages with the most links to them from other highly relevant web pages must be the most relevant pages associated with the search, Page and Brin tested their thesis as part of their studies and laid the foundation for their search engine.

The Google search engine attracted a loyal following among the growing number of Internet users, who liked its simple design and useful results.

My view is:

- You can't run a 'great' hotel if you don't love dealing with people.
- You can't be a 'great' accountant if you don't enjoy making sense of complicated figures.
- You can't be a 'great' local council employee unless you have a strong desire to make people's lives better in your area.
- You can't run a 'great' website unless you can clearly see how your offer will add value to the world and make people's lives easier.

You can survive and even be quite 'successful', but you'll never be 'great', (and your life won't be fulfilling either).

The key to success is to:

**Know what you love to do and
find a way to get paid doing it**

Knowing what you love to do is step 1. Finding a way to get paid to do it is step 2.

This is true for both organisations and individuals. So, if we do have a great Customer Focused Mission (CFM), then what do we mean by the 'customer's real needs'? This is step two. Think about your own experience as a customer. What are your REAL needs in any transaction?

Here are some ideas:

Service or Product	Traditional view of customer's need	Real view of customer's need
Restaurant.	High quality food, great service and atmosphere at sensible prices.	Enjoyment / safe place to meet / an occasion to remember.
Hammer.	High quality at sensible price.	Hammering a nail in easily.
Accountant.	Best advice and accuracy, all delivered on time and in budget.	Trust and partnership.
Landlord.	Good quality accommodation in good location at a fair rent .	Trust, support and safety.

So, **we're not actually selling what we think we're selling** (and we'll talk more about this in Chapter Two). The basic idea is that, when we have that clear Mission and we clearly understand the customer's REAL need, we will then SEE the situation very differently, which in turn will empower and drive us to DO the right things to deliver what we promised.

The horse is now thirsty

With a thirsty horse, we need to provide water (and very often, the horse will find it for itself - so the better you do the first two steps the easier the third and fourth will become).

This is step 3: Go the extra inch.

I use this expression on purpose for the following reasons. The expression 'go the extra mile' is commonly used and abused almost as much as the word 'Mission'. As an employee, if I'm not 100% motivated it means nothing, in fact it's just annoying. If I am 100% motivated it still seems daunting.

'Going the extra mile' is just too far and too unsustainable.

So, 'going the extra inch' is empowering and easy ('by the yard it's hard, by the inch it's a synch'), which is what we want, because let's face it:

- If I cut you in half you wouldn't have the name of your organisation etched through you like a stick of rock would you?
- And neither will any of your employees.

We do a job for what's in it for us, not for the love of it. What could be in it for us will vary dramatically:

- If it's just money, then our service may be shallow to say the least.
- If it is 'love' of the role (just ask anyone who works for a charity), service might be excellent, but the delivery of results can be harder to achieve.

Here's a great news story from the BBC in 2008 which illustrates many of the enigmas and opportunities in this area.

Nurses are to be rated according to the levels of care and empathy they give to patients under government plans.

Health Secretary Alan Johnson told the Guardian newspaper that he wants the performance of every nursing team in England to be scored. He said he believes compassionate care was as crucial to the recovery of patients as the skills of surgeons. Nurse leaders welcomed the move and said they would work with ministers on developing the system.

Mr Johnson said plans were to be outlined in the forthcoming review of the NHS by health minister Lord Darzi. He suggested the results, compiled by regulators using patient surveys, could be displayed on an official website. But he ruled out rating individual nurses and also said it would not affect pay. Standards of nutritional care, minimisation of pain, hand-washing, and safety on the wards could also be measured, he added. Mr Johnson said he hoped to encourage friendly rivalry between wards over which nursing team could achieve the best ratings. The scheme will be piloted and the first results are likely to emerge next year.

Compassion: Mr Johnson said: "What nurses tell us is that you can have the best surgeon in the world, who carries out the most terrific operation on you, but your stay in hospital won't be satisfactory if you don't get a high level of compassion and care. If your experience involves nurses looking grumpy, or someone being rude, or not getting people there when you need them, then it ruins the whole experience."

Wow! It looks like this idea is already catching on!

'Go the extra inch' is based on the fact that most organisations deliver mundane and acceptable levels of service. Most could have the motto, 'we're no worse than anyone else'. In fact our whole society is based around everyone doing the same. It's very threatening when we have people who are talented, not interested in what's 'normal' and who are not prepared to 'do as they're told' (just ask any teacher).

Yet these are just the people who seem to go ahead and make roaring successes of their lives. How can we use this knowledge to empower people?

Well, if this little phrase 'go the extra inch' just gets organisations and individuals to go slightly out of their 'comfort zone' to deliver that little bit extra to the customer, this would motivate and empower people without them becoming dangerous mavericks. Also, because levels of service are so universally mundane and commonplace, if we can actually achieve that 'extra inch' consistently, we'll be head and shoulders above the rest (just ask any athlete).

Once all this is aligned and in place, we'll have a:

- Clear direction (Mission),
- attractive products or services (customer needs), and
- empowered and motivated people (going the extra inch).

It's quite likely, is it not, that this will result in success through

Great levels of customer service excellence

The next question is: how do we keep it there? This is step 4.

In his groundbreaking book 'Good to Great', author Jim Collins, found in a study of around 1,500 US Companies that only 11 were able to sustain superior (3 x average stock market) growth over the long term (15 years). Why was this? There were many reasons (well explained in the book), but, basically it was because the ingredients that made up this excellence usually weren't systemised, so were unsustainable over the long term.

[Note: 'Good to Great' is an excellent book and anyone wanting to improve his or her individual performance and that of their organisation should read and re read it for valuable guidance, facts and insight to enable them to achieve this.]

From the perspective of customer service, the simplest and most effective system to put in place is a basic customer service measure. I call this the **'great or poor measure'**, and we'll look at it in Chapter Two of Section Three.

This approach works, because **what gets measured gets done**, as highlighted in the above article on nurses.

Here's a true story to illustrate all these points.

In the UK a few years ago, there was a small village pub that was quietly going bankrupt due to lack of customers. It wasn't a 'bad' operation, but it was 'no better than any other pub'. It did food (averagely), had an average range of drinks and had a few teams. But, despite having only one member of staff, it couldn't pay the bills and the landlord was foreclosing on overdue rent (which had already been reduced).

This was not a happy situation, but was all too common.

Two business partners had had their eye on this property for a while because they thought it was a great location with potential to do significantly better than it was doing at the time, but they weren't in a position to do anything about it, because they had other occupations and interests.

Just at the time when this pub was on the verge of going under, their other interests finished, so they made an offer to buy the lease of the pub. Their offer was accepted and the deal duly happened (which enabled the ex-owners to pay off all their debts and depart gracefully).

The reason the two business partners bought a lease that was basically worth nothing, was because they had a VISION. There were too many pubs offering mediocre food at high prices - the only alternative was cheap food at cheap prices. They knew that when they wanted to go out, they couldn't think of anywhere decent that wouldn't cost and arm and a leg to go to.

Luckily, both partners were long term passionate pub advocates. Not necessarily because this was a great way to make money, but because they loved everything that pubs stood for (i.e. community, enjoyment, tradition, quality and informality). They had experience in this arena and they genuinely wanted to provide a great place for people to go out to in the wider community. A Customer Focused VISION.

They decided to spend time on a Customer Focused MISSION and VALUES in order to make that VISION live and after much deliberation between themselves, they decided that if they achieved that VISION all their customers would:

Leave with a smile on their face keen to return.

So this became their Customer Focused MISSION. All strategy and processes were then relatively easy to put in place, because the only question to be asked was:

Would this contribute to customers leaving with a smile on their face keen to return?

All staff contracts and training started with the phrase: "The purpose of this is to help you contribute to customers leaving with a smile on their face keen to return".

This was empowering and enlivening. All personnel from chef to bottle washer knew what they needed to DO in order to achieve this. The partners didn't need to tell them because they SAW it clearly!

The partners took a gamble. They stopped the teams from coming (the only real income that was there), spent a reasonable amount on decorations and new equipment and changed the whole direction to one of providing high quality, homemade food at reasonable prices.

But lots of places do this, so they thought:

What does the customer really want? (Focusing on the customer's real needs)

After extensive research, and from extensive experience they decided the following:

- High quality homemade food isn't enough.
- Customers want a great experience.
- They want it at a price that means they can have it regularly.
- It must be consistent so they can tell all their friends and bring business acquaintances along as well.

So the stakes had to be raised. They took a gamble. They thought that the need for the above overrode ALL OTHER CONSIDERATIONS, so they decided not to give a wide choice, not to offer snacks, but only to offer one thing and to offer it brilliantly.

That one thing was: Two course meals, all homemade, at sensible prices. It worked!

When they did this they also went the extra inch by:

- Training all staff on excellent service.
- Clarifying and training VALUES to deliver the MISSION.
- Empowering staff to take whatever action was needed to deliver them.
- Sourcing all food fresh every day.
- Buying well, so they could deliver great quality for sensible prices.
- Linking the wine offer to the food offer (again at sensible prices).
- Offering homemade sweets.
- Ensuring the drinks were also of the highest quality (but not the widest range) and also at sensible prices.

The first eight months were great and the partners were too busy to think about anything else, but then growth stopped (but didn't fall away). What was going wrong?

The answer:: They weren't measuring and by their own standards had become complacent and had lacked innovation. If they weren't careful, turnover would start to fall.

So they introduced the **'great or poor measure'**, initially by asking customers face to face, then by introducing a simple card system.

This resulted in:

- A clear score.
- Enlivening and empowering feedback for partners and staff.
- Direction on what could be done to improve the business.
- More engaged customers.
- An improving turnover.

All the above resulted in > 1000% increase in turnover and, amazingly, this was achieved at a time when the UK pub industry was undergoing the greatest challenge since the First World War.

This is not an 'isn't this fantastic' story, it's simply here to illustrate how the above factors, put into place properly and applied with integrity, have the power to transform even the most traditional business and even in times of economic turmoil.

I know this works. The question is, have you the courage, support and stamina to make the changes needed?

We'll offer you as much help as we can in the next chapters.

I don't know this story so well, but it seems that the founder of Ebay, Pierre Omidyar, went through a similar process when he was starting out. And what is it that makes Ebay so effective?

**Measurement
in the form of
feedback**

Could this be telling us something?

Chapter Two: Customer Focused Mission

"Our deepest fear is not that we are inadequate. Our deepest fear is that we are powerful beyond measure. It is our light, not our darkness that most frightens us. We ask ourselves: "Who am I to be brilliant, gorgeous, talented, and fabulous?" Actually, who are you not to be? You are a child of God. Your playing small doesn't serve the world. There's nothing enlightened about shrinking so that other people won't feel insecure around you. We are all meant to shine, as children do. We were born to make manifest the glory of God that is within us. It's not just in some of us, it's within everyone and as we let our own light shine, we subconsciously give other people permission to do the same." Nelson Mandela at his inaugural speech.

With an outstanding Customer Focused Mission, not only will everyone know what they need to achieve, but also what they need to do to contribute to it.

The purpose of this chapter is to help you achieve one.

There are five steps and apply either individually or organisationally:

We need to know:

1. What we love doing.
2. What we're great at naturally.
3. How we can combine these to make money.
4. How we can ensure this is something that others can 'buy in' to.
5. If we did all this, what would a customer say about us to their friends?

We'll look at all five steps in turn, then I've produced some questions for you to ask yourself both personally and organisationally. This then can be the start of the CFM for you and your organisation.

Please do actually take some action: individually and organisationally. Without getting this right, the roots of excellence in customer service won't be strong and you cannot start your journey to greatness.

Remember:

Knowledge without action is nothing.

Before we start on the steps, it's worth reminding ourselves what the Mission is here for.

A well constructed Mission:

- Tells us what we're here for.
- Is based on a clear and compelling Vision.
- Gives purpose and direction to personnel and decisions.
- Is usually supported by clear values.

Without this, our life (individually) or our organisation will be like a ship at sea without a chart and compass. To use the modern analogy, it's our satellite navigation system.

And please note: a Mission does not need to be a grand thing applying to a whole organisation. Although every organisation needs one (and indeed has one whether they know it or not), it can and does apply at all levels in the organisation and indeed the wider society. To:

- Departments
- Work groups
- Projects
- Teams
- Communities
- Families
- And, of course, you

In turn then and (focused on customer service):

1. What do we love doing?

Individually	Organisationally
What did we love doing as a child?	**What do we love doing?**
We are all just overgrown children. It's wonderful to see the delight of children as they discover and enjoy new things, but how often has this all been lost from about the age of 11. This is when:	What is it in our organisation that we all talk about at social meetings with energy and vigour? What do we look forward to in the week, and what keeps us awake at night excited and enlivened with ideas and possibilities?
<ul><li>We decide it's 'not cool' to be enthusiastic.</li><li>Teachers and parents just want us to do as we're told.</li><li>Our friends are scathing about anything 'out of the ordinary'.</li></ul>	If this is 'most of the things we do', we've every chance of creating a GREAT CFM, and becoming a GREAT organisation.
And when we get our first job, we succumb to the dreaded disease of 'terminal professionalism', so much so that, when many people retire they literally lose the will to live.	We need to work out how we can get rid of what's holding us back from this great Nirvana, swamping us in the bog of mediocrity and how we can create more time to doing and developing these wonderful things.
What would we do if we didn't need the income?	There are many stories of great organisations who have thrown off the shackles of past business, focused on what they loved and thought they could be great at, and went on to conquer the world.
Escape from the terminal professionalism, and the illusion that we 'have to' do anything!	
Start dreaming constructively, and then planning the great escape. **If we are not doing what we love we will NEVER be great at it.**	**How would we, as a group of people, run this organisation if we weren't paid?**
	The acid test. If the answer is 'not the things we're being paid to do now', then we've really got a problem! It's never too late to change.
	Unfortunately, all too often, people within organisations allow money to 'pollute' their integrity in their activity (just look at the recent tragedy of sub-prime loans).
	True success ONLY comes when you do what's right, the money then follows - not the other way round.

Individually	Organisationally
What would we want to say on our death bed? I've asked this question hundreds of times and it's never: • "At least I made budget", or • "Thank God I got that new car", etc. It's always about values, and what's 'worthwhile'. Your Mission must reflect this. **Who and what inspires us?** What can we learn about ourselves from this? Will it help us find our Mission (note 'find' not 'create' - I believe there's a Mission inside each of us, we just need to put time and effort into discovering it, and it probably won't happen overnight). Why are some people so motivated, calm and inspiring? It's usually because, whether they know it or not, they've found their Mission and found how they can get paid to do it. JOY! What hobbies do we have? Do they hold clues to what we could be GREAT at? (Imagine being paid to do your hobby every day!) **What do we 'feel alive' when doing?** We know when we're alive, when work seems easy, time just flies by and problems are just trivialities. This often happens in love, on the first hour of a holiday, with great friends and of course when we're doing what we were made to do (often called being in 'flow'). If this happens when we're serving people in our jobs, then we know we're in the right jobs, and we've every chance of becoming GREAT at them. **If we had $1m that we had to give to charity, which charity would we give it to and why?** This will provide some real pointers. And don't forget, your TIME is worth much more than any money! How do you REALLY want to spend it?	**At a colleagues' reunion in 20 years time, what would we laugh about and slap each other on the backs over and over again for?** Not the howlers. The great things. • The accountants who enabled a small business to prosper. • The hospital that had the highest recovery rate. • The pub that had those consistently happy customers. • The Hotel that won the awards and had 90% customer retention. • The manufacturer that invented and perfected a new product that made a real difference to people's lives. This is not about money: it's about what matters. **What would make our customers describe us as 'GREAT' (not just 'good')?** How can we focus our talents and resources on what really matters: i.e.: • Adding value to the world • Making a difference to people's lives • Helping other people prosper and flourish **If we had to support a charity by law, which one would it be and why?** This will show you what your organisation's true values are.

2. What are we great at naturally?

Individually	Organisationally
What do other people say we're 'good' at?	**What does the 'man on the street' say about our services?**

What do other people say we're 'good' at?

The opposite of this seems to be an obsession for many people today, but we need to turn this on its head and discover (by honesty and genuinely asking - and not being afraid of poor feedback), what we're great at, and what we aren't. Using a life coach helps enormously with this.

99% of people die 'with their music inside them'. This is a book subject on its own, but so often we only learn the great aspects about people we know, when we hear someone speaking at their funeral!

What do we 'feel alive' doing?
See above.

What's working well in our life?

- What do people like about us?
- What great things have we done?
- What disasters have we experienced that will help guide us through future issues (so often great tragedies transform
  individuals to release themselves from their shackles and enable them to excel).
- What unique experiences and talents do we have that can produce benefit in the future?

What's not?

- What causes us frustration and stress?
- What do we want to be good at but simply aren't?
- What are we doing because of social pressure, that we'd really rather not?
- What are we ashamed of?

What natural talents, experience and skills do we possess that mean we can excel at something?

We are all unique and each of us has natural talents. Our natural talents and skills mean that we can achieve some aim that no-one else can. And what if this life is just one of many in a continuing stream?

What does the 'man on the street' say about our services?

This is the one key question I would always ask customers who wanted help, when I was a Director of a large Pub Company in the UK.

If they could tell me, then I'd be interested in helping them. If they didn't, what was the point?

This is the single most important question we can ask about our organisations. It's also the question 99% of organisations haven't a clue about. They do 'satisfaction surveys', ask the questions they want nswers to, and then kid themselves that everything's 'fine'. No it isn't.

What about all the issues 'between the lines' and the 90% of customers who they haven't asked?

This hugely important question will be addressed in Section Three.

What would we want him or her to say?

A bit of a 'chicken and egg' situation maybe. Until we know what he or she IS saying, we might not know what we'd want him or her to say.

Apart from this, we've seen examples pointless Mission statements. I believe that if the Mission statement addresses this single question, then it's probably in the right area.

Customers don't care about shareholder return or 'being the leading' this or that, they just care about whether their needs have been met (or preferably exceeded) and do I trust these people, and have they made my life better and easier?

In short:

- The customer is KING
- The customer's view is the LAW

Individually	Organisationally
If we could turn back time, what would we change?	**What energises this organisation?**
We stress and fuss about this constantly, yet we cannot change anything.	This links above: what are we naturally good at (because of Vision, direction, personalities, organisation, values, skills, experience geography etc.)
The only time we have is the present.	
So, we've all made howlers in the past: What good can we glean from them?	If people aren't energised by something, they'll NEVER be great at it.
What can we learn about ourselves and what motivates us?	**What saps our energy?**
	There'll be no problem finding this out! Most meetings focus on this almost exclusively. The point is - what can we learn to stop doing and how can we re-direct our energies into doing something we would be great at?
	What natural position, skills and experience do we possess that means we could be the best in the world at something? Consider:
	• History
	• Geography
	• Skills
	• Values
	• Successes
	• Patents
	Then put your mind on another plane, forget this all for its own sake and try and put yourself in the mindset of a complete outsider.
	Considering all the above, what could we really do that would be hugely successful if we really put our minds to it?
	What can we learn from past mistakes that would help us improve?
	We stress and fuss about this constantly in organisations, yet we cannot change anything.
	The only time we have is the present.
	We can use past mistakes to plan and train for a more successful future, and we can ask ourselves: what unique problems have we overcome that'll help us become GREAT at something in the future?

3. How can we combine these to make money?

Individually	Organisationally

This point works equally well for the individual and the organisation.

Money is a result, NOT a cause

- of a Mission
- of a lifetime
- of value given

Money without a worthwhile cause is a cancer and will eventually destroy you (mentally if not physically). Money with a worthwhile cause is a huge blessing that enables you to do all sorts of extra things.

This is simple: you either believe this or you don't. It's not up to me, it's up to you. My view is you'll see it when you believe it, not believe it when you see it. Success is finding out what you could be GREAT at and then finding a way to be paid to do it.

I'd just like to illustrate my point with two examples in each category from recent history. The first is money not based on a worthwhile cause, the second is the other way round. The amount of money is irrelevant.

Robert Maxwell:	Enron

Robert Maxwell:

Here's an extract from Wikipedia.

Maxwell's death triggered a flood of revelations about his controversial business dealings and activities. It emerged that, without adequate prior authorisation, he had used hundreds of millions of pounds from his companies' pension funds to finance his corporate debt, his frantic takeovers and his lavish lifestyle.

Thousands of Maxwell employees lost their pensions. The Maxwell companies filed for bankruptcy protection in 1992. His sons, Kevin Maxwell and Ian Maxwell, were declared bankrupt with debts of £400 million.

In 1995 the two Maxwell sons and two other former directors went on trial for fraud, but were acquitted in 1996. In 2001 the Department of Trade and Industry report on the collapse of the Maxwell companies accused both Maxwell and his sons of acting "inexcusably".

It came to light in early 2006 that, before his death, Maxwell was being investigated for possible war crimes in Germany in 1945. This led to renewed speculation that his death was a suicide.

An interesting legacy to leave after a lifetime of graft!

Enron

Another one from Wikipedia.

Enron Corporation was an American energy company based in Houston, Texas. Before its bankruptcy in late 2001, Enron employed around 22,000 people and was one of the world's leading electricity, natural gas, pulp and paper, and communications companies, with claimed revenues of $111 billion in 2000.

Fortune named Enron "America's Most Innovative Company" for six consecutive years. At the end of 2001 it was revealed that its reported financial condition was sustained substantially by Institutionalised, systematic, and creatively planned accounting fraud.

Enron has since become a popular symbol of wilful corporate fraud and corruption.

An interesting symbol to create!

Mother Teresa

Here's an extract from CNN on her death

Mother Teresa's tireless efforts on behalf of world peace brought her a number of important humanitarian awards, including the Nobel Peace Prize in 1979. She said such earthly rewards were important only if they helped her help the world's needy.

"Pray together and we stay together, and if we stay together, we'll love each other as God himself loves you," Mother Teresa once said.

The small nun with the large heart worked tirelessly to the very end, despite illness in her later years. She was hospitalised in early 1996 after breaking her collarbone in a fall at her Calcutta headquarters.

And here's what she said about 'money' and 'service':

> "Be faithful in small things because it is in them that your strength lies."

> "Even the rich are hungry for love, for being cared for, for being wanted, for having someone to call their own."

> "God doesn't require us to succeed - he only requires that we try."

> "I try to give to the poor people for love what the rich could get for money."

> "No, I wouldn't touch a leper for a thousand pounds, yet I willingly cure him for the love of God."

> "If you can't feed a hundred people, then feed just one."

Merck

Here's the first paragraph from their website

Merck & Co., Inc. is a global research-driven pharmaceutical company dedicated to putting patients first. Established in 1891, Merck discovers, develops, manufactures and markets vaccines and medicines to address unmet medical needs.

The company devotes extensive efforts to increase access to medicines through far reaching programs that not only donate Merck medicines but help deliver them to the people who need them. Merck also publishes unbiased health information as a not-for-profit service.

Who wouldn't want to work for or do business with them?

What a great and lasting legacy.

4. How can we ensure that this is something that others can buy into?

Individually	Organisationally
What will show that I mean it?	**What will show that I mean it?**

Individually

What will show that I mean it?

Actions speak louder than words:

What can I do to show I mean it? We all make promises and have good intentions, but, when push comes to shove, if we don't start changing our habits, our intentions mean nothing.

The worst time to make an intention to change a habit is about 12.05 am on 1st January (which is the only time when 99% of people do it). Why? Because it's based on false will.

The only way you'll make a change is by spending time, a lot of time, discovering your answers to the above questions, and reflecting on what REALLY matters to you.

And then DOING something different.

As a professional man, I always said I wanted to be a great father, yet I would perpetually miss appointments, get home late, and be 'too tired' to play at the weekends. Not much point in the intention then. When I realised this wasn't a very effective fathering strategy, I spent time considering how I could change. I had some fantastic help from various sources, but, I decided three things:

- I would plan my week with my role as father being a role of prime importance.
- When arriving home, I would ask myself 'what would a 'GREAT' father (and husband) do when arriving home?
- I would involve my family in these decisions and ask them to hold me accountable.

It's really made a difference.

Organisationally

What will show that I mean it?

This is crucial in organisations.

Mission statements have had bad press for a reason, and it's this: if you don't mean it don't say it.

If you've got the foresight and guts to spend time and effort on getting a Mission right, you HAVE TO ensure that you stick to it, come rain or shine, no matter what.

The minute you deviate, no matter how extreme the circumstances, is the minute you lose it.

And all your hard work and good intentions go out of the window.

A reputation takes a lifetime to earn and a minute to destroy.

Your reputation is linked to how you stick to your Mission.

Proof that you mean it:

- Amazon.com will tell you where you can buy products cheaper (and not necessarily from them).

- Ebay lives or dies on feedback (a separate and very important issue in itself that we'll come back to).

- Supermarkets that give 200% guarantees on their products.

- Consultants that say 'if we don't add value to you, then we don't expect you to pay' (wouldn't that be great!)

This is achieved by having:

- Strategy, processes and behavioural measures that are clearly linked to the Mission.
- Guarantees, and service charters that enshrine this in black and white.
- Empowered people who stick by this no matter what.

Individually	Organisationally
Some top tips to 'prove you mean it':	But what happens all too often is:

Individually

Some top tips to 'prove you mean it':

- Spend time getting the Mission statement right.

- Share it with those that matter to you.

- Ask them for input.

- Ask them to hold you accountable.

- Ask yourself, before you do anything: does this add to or take away from my Mission.

Remember the devil is often in the detail (get the small things right, and the big things often take care of themselves).

Remember to be strong in the hard moments (this is when the real tests happen).

Whether other people agree with you or not, is not the issue. People can only 'buy into you' if you're clear on your Mission, and all your actions reflect this.

And you're big enough to admit it and say sorry when they don't.

A big challenge!

If you do stick to your guns, like minded people will gravitate towards you, and you'll find support and succour where you least expected it.

Organisationally

But what happens all too often is:

- Companies that say they're the cheapest but hide behind 'extras'.

- Hotels that treat you like a number, then ask for your feedback on poxy cards (which they obviously never read).

- Consultants who charge you no matter whether they've made a difference or not.

- Police forces that measure arrests made and completed paperwork rather than crime reduction and enhanced welfare of the community.

- People who say they'll ring you back, but 'forget' (my biggest gripe - it's so easy to get right, but so pathetic how few people do).

**The Mission drives EVERYTHING
Or it drives NOTHING**

If you do stick to your Mission, not only will you attract people to your organisation that want to be part of the same thing, but also, those already with you will either change to conform (readily and willingly) or start to find somewhere else to go.

Either is the right outcome.

5. If we did all this, what would a customer say about us to their friends?

This is the fruit of getting the first four questions right. The future success, or otherwise of our business <u>depends</u> on what people say about you behind your back.

So it's essential to be clear what you think this should be. And this will form the basis of your Customer Focused Mission.

This is such a hard question to ask yourself or your organisation, so simply try this:

1. Make a list of your views (see the questions following).

2. Ask as many colleagues, friends and customers as possible for their views.

3. Sit down and review this with your people.

4. Clarify and distil it all with a disinterested party.

This is too important to get wrong .... take your time.

Success or failure as a human being or organisation is not a matter of luck, circumstances, fate, or any of the other tiresome old clichés. Those are only excuses. The power to achieve the life of your dreams is in your hands and the first step toward activating it is identifying the Mission statement that will make your dreams real. After all, it's only possible to get what you want out of life when you know where you're going!

A Mission statement is only a SHORT statement, but it has specific, measurable outcomes. It's truly the best way to start your journey to success. The following questions make it easy for you to put your Mission statement together in a simple, step-by-step, ten-minute process.

Spend the time on this NOW! You won't do it later.

Jim Rohn said, "You cannot change your destination overnight, but you can change your direction overnight." Creating a Mission statement will help you change your direction. In just ten minutes from now, you will have made the shift from an ordinary existence to an extraordinary existence.

INDIVIDUAL

Take the following steps:

Find yourself somewhere quiet where you won't be disturbed no matter what (many people do this in the car - it helps if you drive to somewhere peaceful and scenic, and not the centre of Birmingham).

- Turn off all electronic communicative apparatus.
- Inhale deeply, counting to 5.
- Exhale counting to 10.
- Repeat until you feel calm and relaxed.

Now, take 10 minutes to answer these questions as quickly and honestly as you can. Don't worry about the answers, just do it quickly, you'll get closest to the truth this way.

INDIVIDUAL

What did I love doing as a child?

What would I do if I didn't need the income?

What would I want to say on my death bed?

Who and what inspire me?

What hobbies do I have?

What do I 'feel alive' when doing?

If I had £1m that I had to give to charity, which charity would I give it to and why?

What do other people say I'm 'good' at?

What's working well in my life?

What's not?

What natural talents, experience and skills mean I can be best in the world at something?

If I could turn back time, what would I change?

What things are not done well by other people that I could be GREAT at?

Where is the world moving in the future, and what skills and talents will be needed?

What would a GREAT (insert most important role, i.e., mother, father, manager, wife, etc) do?

What would a GREAT (insert second most important role) do?

What would a GREAT (insert third most important role) do?

What's so important to me that I must do it no matter what?

Now: circle 3 to 5 things that you feel most strongly about and write them again here.

Now, start mulling over in your mind: "if I did all these, what would people say about me?" Write some responses here:

Now you have the basis of a Customer Focused Mission statement. Use this space to draw and expand on this, when you feel calm and creative. Eventually you will discover the right words over time if you persist, ask other people, put time aside, and really WANT to do this.

ORGANISATIONAL

Take the following steps (which may take some significant time - that's fine, it's worth doing and it's worth doing well):

1. Plan some time to address these questions on your own, about two weeks in the future.
2. Send some of these questions out to colleagues to gain their views.
3. Schedule a brainstorming meeting with them 48 hours after your own scheduled time (make sure it's done at a 'calm' time of year, when no other pressing deadlines are distracting the participants).
4. Take the time you've allocated to collate responses and put down some thoughts in the format shown below.
5. Have the brainstorming meeting.
   a It's vital to explain WHY you're doing this (use the above material in your own words).
   b Tell them that you'd really value their input.
   c Tell them what you'll do with it.
   d Have the meeting (keep it short and fun).
6. Prioritise the output and circulate it.
7. Reconvene and refine.
8. Agree roles and desired results, and start implementation.
9. Meet regularly on this subject (alone) to refine and adjust.

What do we love doing?

How would we, as a group of people, run this organisation if we weren't paid?

At a colleagues' reunion in 20 years time, what would we laugh about and slap each other on the backs over and over again for?

What would make our customers describe us as 'GREAT' (not just 'good')?

If we had to support a charity by law, which one would it be and why?

What does the 'man on the street' say about our services?

What would we want him or her to say?

What energises this organisation?

What saps our energy?

What natural position, skills and experience do we possess that means we could be the best in the world at something?

What can we learn from past mistakes that would help us improve?

What are others not good at that we could naturally be GREAT at?

Where will the market we are in be in 10 or 20 years time?

What would our service or product look like if it was PERFECT from a customer's point of view?

What are the most important things that our people value?

What are the most important things that our community value?

What things are so important that they should be done whether or not they make money?

If we went bust tomorrow, what great things would we be remembered for?

What could we do in the future that would 'make a worthwhile difference'?

If we did all this, what would a customer say about us to their friends?

Note: if the above seems daunting, or you've already got a Mission and have been trading for a while, don't panic. It's never too late to change, but don't try and do it all at once. Take it slowly, involve senior managers first and eventually involve everyone - it will start to evolve and flourish.

As the Chinese proverb goes:

"The best time to plant a tree is 40 years ago. The second best time is today."

And remember: Doing this takes guts and dedication. This won't be an 'overnight success'. Indeed, you'll get setbacks and resistance at every turn. But don't despair, simply by spending time on this, you'll be putting yourself in the top 5% of the population, and you'll be on your way to spending time with the likes of Amazon and Merck, rather than Enron and Robert Maxwell. It's got to be worth a bit of bother!

Here's a quote from Sydney Harbour Bridge Visitor Centre:

"Work was demanding and dangerous, but workers felt a special camaraderie and shared a sense of pride. Everyone was aware of the fact that the project would stand or fall on the basis of the quality and precision of their workmanship."

What a great simile for customer service work in every organisation today. Your job is to get this kind of atmosphere and commitment within your organisation. Getting the CFM right is the first and most important step in achieving this.

We started with a quote, so we'll finish with two:

"A business leader has to keep their organisation focused on the Mission. That sounds easy, but it can be tremendously challenging in today's competitive and ever-changing business environment. A leader also has to motivate potential partners to join" Meg Whitman, CEO of Ebay.

And remember

"The man who sticks to his plan, becomes the man he used to want to be."

Chapter Three: The Customer's Real Needs

"To my customer: I may not have the answer, but I'll find it. I may not have the time, but I'll make it. I may not be the biggest, but I'll be the most committed to your success."

"When the customer comes first, the customer will last."

"A sale is not something you pursue, it's what happens to you while you are immersed in serving your customer."

The heading of this chapter says it all. Focus on the customer's:

Needs and desires.

Obvious? Well, yes, and, no. The question is:

How do we know what the customer's needs and desires really are?

Because,

if we don't, then we can't focus on them, even if we wanted to.

Which stands to reason. It would be churlish to suggest that most organisations don't try to do this (though there are some), but all so often, they miss the mark. So why is this? The reason is very simple:

Organisations see themselves from the inside out,

But

Customers see them from the outside in.

So it's exactly like two sides of the coin. Both see each other completely differently. Have you ever noticed as a customer you can see all the issues that need resolving in an organisation as clear as a bell, but if you then join that organisation, the clarity disappears overnight. Your perception has changed (and they're paying your mortgage).

The key to effective self and organisational management is to maintain the 'outside in' perspective, when you're operating from the inside out. Very hard to do.

Here are some tips on how to do it:

- Customer surveying: see Section Three.
- Regular meetings with key customers, use their agenda, not yours.
- Seek out and face facts (Churchill was excellent at this in the Second World War).
- Deal with everything objectively: leave out the ego and emotion.
- Checks and balances.

Here's a simple diagram to illustrate the point:

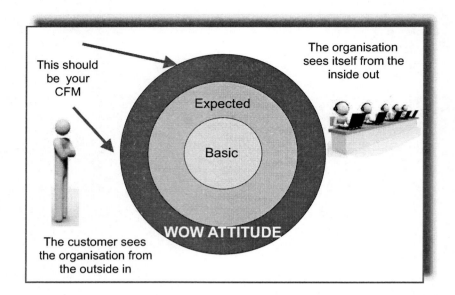

This becomes doubly complicated when we consider that the customer's real needs and desires are also 'hidden'. i.e.:

Customers hold their desires inside,

But

Organisations only see the external results of those desires.

So, in effect, they have to base their judgment on what they think a customer 'really wants', on guesswork. Every customer has different internal needs and desires and they manifest these externally in different ways.

This is an area of constant research and market analysis. Indeed the whole of the marketing and advertising industry is built around researching, meeting (and more importantly, influencing) these internal needs, fears and desires. So much so in fact, that our true needs, fears and desires have to a significant extent been manipulated and subjugated by the power of marketing, to become conformist (and frankly, alarmingly dull and lemming-like).

The principle behind this chapter works at many levels:

1st level: the basics:

Do your research really well, and move with the times.

- It's irrelevant if you're passionate about your creation if no-one wants it. (Remember the Sinclair C5?)
- You have to anticipate and move with change in your market. (E.g: There's little success to be found selling and promoting traditional cameras and film in the digital age.)

This is just the 'starting point' for businesses.

2nd Level: the 'choice':

You can't please all the people all the time. You have to choose your market and be prepared to say 'no' to the people who don't fit into it! For example

- You won't put a pool table into a quality restaurant.
- Don't ask your Accountant to do your sales forecast.
- And don't try and buy a Pizza in McDonalds!

This is where good businesses build brand and identity. I do not intend to spend time on analysis of these. Organisations must do their market research properly. The real issue I intend to promote is:

3rd Level: the 'emotion', the Moments of Truth that link the customers' REAL emotions to our Customer Focused Mission. This is the focus of this chapter.

Getting this right empowers our Organisation towards world class success. Here's a diagram to illustrate:

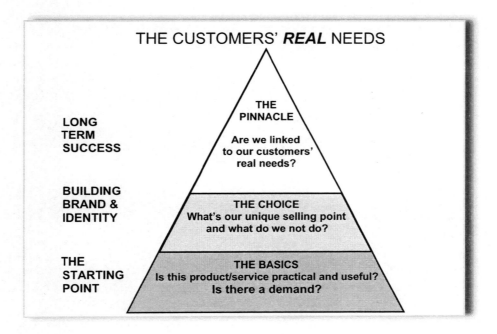

This can sound daunting … customers have many different emotions and are completely unpredictable. But we have some good news for you. The answer to this, like everything that's been properly thought through and is designed to actually work, is deceptively simple. Your customers' REAL needs are generally a mix of two simple and blindingly obvious things.

Customers only REALLY want two things
1. **Trust**
2. **Life to be easier**

The world is changing. The Internet is and will empower the customer unlike anything before it. Marketing and advertising will start to be less influential as customers regain their consciousness and share customer focused feedback amongst themselves and to the world at large.

The writing is on the wall.

- Customers can no longer be influenced and hoodwinked on such a massive scale. (Just see the current movements for fair trade and sustainability).

- Customers really are king
  - Listening to them is powerful.
  - Anticipating and responding to their needs and desires based upon their feedback is world-beating.

Organisations must spend less on marketing and advertising (remember how much more it costs to gain a new customer versus retaining an existing one), and MUCH MORE on:

- Listening PROPERLY to customers.
- Finding out their real needs and desires.
- Anticipating future needs and desires.
- Reorganising around these needs and desires.
- Going the extra inch.

Whenever I talk to 'business consultants', they spend a lot of time talking about marketing, trade building and promotions but seldom talk about the above. Perhaps it's too simple and obvious. Perhaps it won't generate lots of fees. I have no idea, but it seems like BOCS to me!

So, in order to be successful in the long term, organisations have to do two things:

1. Organise their organisation from the 'outside in' (the customer's perception).

   a. Shall we call this aligning around a CFM?
   b. Have we covered this enough?

2. Constantly seek out and listen to the customer from the customer's point of view and then develop the organisation around these findings, (keeping the CFM as a compass to guide the development).

We'll learn how to do item 2. above in Section Three of this book, and the rest of this Chapter will focus on the skills to help your organisation **focus on the customer's needs and desires.**

Because remember:

Customers only want two things.
To Trust
and for their life to be better,

Through dealing with you.

So lets' look at these in turn.

1. To Trust

Trust means reliance on the integrity, strength, ability, surety, etc., of a person or thing: Confidence. So, if you can achieve this from your customers, the world is literally your oyster. Yet it's so rare in the world today. Why is this? Because organisations (and people) just can't seem to stop themselves from going for the 'quick win'. One 'quick win' at the expense of the customer, destroys TRUST forever.

Not a very sensible bargain. Yet again BOCS, yet so often not common practice.

Franklin Covey has a wonderful definition of trust.

Trust is a mixture of:

- Competence, and
- Character.

The point is that trust (being the lubrication of success), is built around two precepts. In order to trust you, I must:

- Believe that you'll do what you say you'll do, as well as possible (competence).
- Know that you'll consider my needs as an individual when doing it (character).

Some examples of high competence and low character.

- An accountant might be the best accountant in the world, but I won't trust him or her if they don't return my phone call when they say they will.

- A doctor might be the best at a particular operation in the world, but I won't trust them if I think they're being 'incentivised' by a drug company to prescribe one particular drug over another.

- A jeweller may provide jewellery at the cheapest price in the country, but if the MD describes it as 'total crap' I won't buy it.

- A chef might be the most talented in the world, but if he or she spends time on TV promoting themselves excessively, I might avoid them because I think they're more interested in their ego than their food.

- Politicians … (say no more)

Some examples of high character and low competence.

- My accountant might be a 'jolly nice chap', but if he makes a mistake with my tax return twice, I'll find another one.

- My doctor may be very pleasant company and always cheerful, but if he missed a crucial symptom, then I'll go to someone else next time.

- A jeweller might offer fantastic customer service, but if their prices are well out of kilter with elsewhere (and they have no other distinguishing factor), their business will die.

- A chef may be a great character and passionately devoted to his food, but if he burns my steak twice, I'm likely to eat elsewhere.

- Public bodies and charities often have very high character, but sometimes fail to 'deliver the goods' so to speak.

- People who are great at their 'jobs' but rubbish at organising themselves (so they don't do what they say they will) can't be trusted, even though I want to.

Here's a simple diagram to illustrate this point.

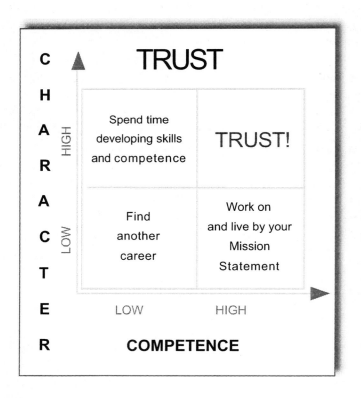

In a nutshell however, here's a simple guide:

SIMPLE GUIDE	
Your Situation	**Your Actions**
Low competence, low character.	Find something to do that you're actually interested in and stop wasting everyone else's time and money.
Low competence, high character.	Well done, you've got the hard bit right. Take some time out to develop competency over and above what's needed.
Low character, high competence.	Alarm bells ringing here. Spend time considering your personal Mission (see above). You need to consider what people would say about you at your funeral if you died tomorrow. Read the story of what Alfred Nobel did with his life. Remember what people currently think of bankers and politicians!
High character, high competence.	Whatever you do, don't rest on your laurels: Success is the first ingredient of failure. Keep your Mission to the fore, keep promoting and rewarding character, keep training for competence and keep ahead of the game. Learn from top sportsmen. They train and develop themselves continuously, even when they're at the top of their tree (it seems ludicrous to suggest otherwise, but just look at what some people and organisations do in reality).

And here are some guidelines of behaviour that can build trust:

Character:

- Prioritise around what's important, rather than what's urgent.
- Listen to others from their point of view.
- Speak well of people behind their back.
- Take responsibility for failure, pass on credit for success.
- Be compassionate.
- Keep commitments.
- Apologise for failures, and take great steps to right them.
- Trust others.
- Subjugate your ego to 'what matters'.
- Be honest.

Competence:

- Keep commitments.
- Commit to perpetual self improvement.
- Seek feedback (and act on it).
- Prioritise around what's important, rather than what's urgent.
- Communicate clearly (based on 'desired results' not 'actions').
- Deliver results.
- Consider the other person's point of view as well as your own.

As previously mentioned, 'The Speed of Trust' by Stephen M.R. Covey is an excellent resource if you want to learn how to build trust.

In essence, however:

A customer just wants to trust you!

And the only way you'll do that is by finding out what they REALLY want and ensuring that you do it, on time every time, fairly.

Who does this well?

- Amazon: not only do they have a huge stock range and completely reliable returns and delivery service (competence), they also tell you where you can get the things at a better price and guarantee everything (character).

- Ebay: here's a clip of a recent article from the BBC.

  'Open forum'

  The feedback forum was introduced by Ebay founder Pierre Omidyar in February 1996. In a message then, he said: "By creating an open market that encourages honest dealings, I hope to make it easier to conduct business with strangers over the net.

  Now, we have an open forum. Use it. Make your complaints in the open.

  Better yet, give your praise in the open. Let everyone know what a joy it was to deal with someone.

  Above all, conduct yourself in a professional manner."

It's ALL founded on TRUST!

So, as the world changes in the future, if you want to delight customers, is it important to consider their needs and desires and act in a competent and considerate way before considering the need for profit?

You bet it is.

2. Making Life 'Easier'.

Supermarkets know this is a key consideration:

- Tesco: 'Every little helps'.
- Sainsbury's: 'Making life taste better'.
- Wal-Mart: 'Save money, live better'.

As Status Quo famously sang:

"Life is hard, I need a remedy: my bread keeps landing jam side down!"

So the last thing anyone needs is for an organisation that's delivering us a service to make life harder for us. If they do, they'll always go out of business in the long term (because if nothing else their customers won't warn them to future changes to their needs). But it still happens so often:

Here are some examples:

- Organisations that own property who forget how to look after their customers, so the quality of their customers falls over time. They don't notice it until it's too late.

- Organisations with a monopoly who don't consider this, will go out of business quicker than a rat out of an aqueduct as soon as competition comes along.

And the most common:

- Organisations who develop policies around their own internal needs (and especially those of the finance department), with little regard as to the perception of these policies in the eyes and experience of the customer.

But most organisations simply don't consider this properly, and so they spend a fortune in time and money trying to promote themselves and grow, but it always seems like 'wading through mud'!

All you really need to do is:

Make life easier for your customers and they'll make life easier for you.

The truly effective lifestyle

So what does 'easier' mean?

The dictionary definition of 'easy' is:

1. Capable of being accomplished or acquired with ease, posing no difficulty: An easy victory, an easy problem.

2. Requiring or exhibiting little effort or endeavour; undemanding: Took the easy way out of her problems; wasn't satisfied with an easy answers.

3. Free from worry, anxiety, trouble, or pain: My mind was easy, knowing that I had done my best.

4. a. Affording comfort or relief; soothing: Soft light that was easy on the eyes.
   b. Prosperous; well-off: Easy living; easy circumstances.

5. Causing little hardship or distress: An easy penalty; a habit that isn't easy to give up.

6. Socially at ease: An easy, good-natured manner.

7. a. Relaxed in attitude; easygoing: An easy disposition.
   b. Not strict or severe; lenient: an easy teacher; easy standards.

8. Readily exploited, imposed on, or tricked: an easy mark; an easy victim.

9. a. Not hurried or forced; moderate: an easy pace; an easy walk around the **block**.
   b. Light; gentle: an easy tap on the shoulder.

10. Not steep or abrupt; gradual: an easy climb.

So, it means quite a lot then!

To simplify this, from a customer service point of view, 'easy' probably means something like this:

- Hassle free
- Reliable
- Pleasant to deal with
- Simple and quick

The most important question is: what does 'easy' mean to our customer?

And in order to answer this we need to remember what business we're in, and what our customers might REALLY be wanting from us.

Business	What might the customer REALLY want	What might make this 'easy' for the customer
Hotel.	Restfulness and comfort.	Quick check in and out, cleanliness, attentive but unobtrusive service.
Accountant.	Reliability and small bills.	Reminders, standardized forms, easy to follow instructions, translating 'tax speak' into plain English
Printing Company.	Reliability, quality and responsiveness at a fair price	Phone updates, guarantees, ease of proofreading, delivery included.
Supermarket.	A wide range at fair prices.	Ease of parking, clear store layout, personalized greeting service, no queues!

So you need to take some time out from your busy bustling agenda and consider (from their point of view, NOT YOURS), what business are we really in, and what would make it 'easy'? Forget considerations on cost or logistics: this is strategy creation for the long term.

If we can visualize something we can generally attain it. It may take huge changes, but what are we here for: to maintain the 'status quo' (beware family companies!), or to progress and grow?

Put some initial thoughts down here:

What business are we really in?

If we had no restrictions at all, how could we make it easier for customers?

What could we do from the above to make it easier now?

What do we need to start developing for the future?

Here's a great example of this done poorly:

> In Sydney Australia, there are three different toll road systems. As a visitor, in order to use these roads (without incurring a fine) you have to log on to and register with the three different Companies who own them. Net result: visitors avoid them and this creates a bad impression of the whole visiting experience.

And don't forget, all of this applies at an individual level too. Do we gravitate towards or away from people who make life harder? (It's worth remembering this when we consider how to deal with difficult people).

So it's easy! All we have to do is build trust and make life 'easy' for our customers.

Yes, it's simple to understand, and that's more than half the battle, but in reality we find it's hard to put into practice, because there are so many dysfunctional attitudes ingrained in us all.

Here are some tips to help:

1. <u>Moments of Truth</u>: Revisit and reconsider your 'Moments of Truth' exercise above. Keep revisiting and reconsidering it.

2. <u>Learn from those who do it well</u> either inside or outside your organisation. What do you like as a customer? What could you learn from and integrate?

3. <u>Service charters guarantees</u>: Create and measure some clear and simple service charters from your customer's point of view. For example: 'If we don't deliver on time, we won't charge you'.

   This benefits both parties:

   a. The customer: reduces anxiety.
   b. The Organisation: forces them to get the process right.
   c. The relationship: builds trust!

4. <u>Organisation</u>: Align all strategies, processes and behaviour measures around the Mission (see above).

5. <u>Training</u>:
   a. Character: The Mission (and values) and (most importantly, but often ignored) why we live it.
   b. Competency: The knowledge & skills needed to do the job excellently.

6. <u>Systems</u>: Doing 'what it says on the tin'!
   a. Doing what you say you'll do promotes trust and makes the customer's life easier.
   b. Not doing this (unless in an exceptional situation, and handled exceptionally), does the opposite.

7. <u>Checks and balances</u>: To make sure the systems are working.

8. <u>Empowerment</u>: To make sure the right behaviour CAN happen.

9. <u>Reward</u>: To reward 'great' behaviour in both employees and customers.

10. <u>Guarantees</u>: To promote trust and accountability, and make life easier for the customer.

We will discuss a lot of this in the next chapter: 'Go the Extra Inch'.

Two other hot tips:

1. First impressions Last a lifetime!

So, whatever you do, make sure you get this right.

Consider:

- Telephone answering.
- Website.
- Vans / lorries.
- Appearance of premises:
    i   Paintwork.
    ii Litter.
    iii Polish.
    iv Signage.
- Appearance of personnel.
- Marketing / advertising.

From the customer's point of view, not yours!

Do they ALL reflect your Mission and Values?

I came across a telephone Company in Australia where, when I phoned the operator for help with making a call to the UK (at great expense) I was met by a series of adverts for their system, before I even had the chance of selecting an option!

2. Simple things done well

This is something I promote endlessly in the pub industry in the UK and it links to the second level of this principle.

It seems to me that many organisations try to do too much and then do it averagely at best. This results in low growth rates and frustration (for all parties).

Whereas we know the customer only wants two things:

1. Trust
2. Easier life

Logically, the best way for any organisation to deliver this is to simplify matters and then focus on doing one or two things brilliantly, rather than lots of things mediocrely.

I also do a fair amount of work with public bodies in the UK and this always seems to be an issue for them. I usually advise them to 'forget' the multiples of measures they are presented with by Central Government and instead, focus on one or two measures that, if done brilliantly, would result in most of the others being achieved as well. This makes their life much easier and energises and motivates people at all levels.

Indeed there was a famous case of an award winning head teacher in the UK putting her success down to 'ignoring all government strategies'.

Ebay is the ultimate embodiment of this strategy.

Simply put:

Simple things done well
are far better than
complicated things done averagely.

CONCLUSION

The conclusion of this Chapter is simple. In order to succeed you MUST find out the customers REAL needs and desires, and then arrange strategies, processes and behaviour around them.

Because:

Your product or service is NOT your business.
The feeling it creates in your customer is!

When you've done business with your customer, you want him or her to look like this.

To finish: I Googled 'what does the customer want?' and got this from www.justsell.com as my first hit, which sums it up nicely!

"Customer service is a sales opportunity."

To improve service is to improve the experience at each and every point of interaction that customers and prospects have with your company. Remember, quality customer service is defined by the individual experiencing it. One size, one solution does not always work. Buyers want to be treated as unique individuals. However, companies renowned for their customer service know that one can orchestrate or create a customer service experience that most often exceeds customers' expectations.

What does the customer want at this moment?

What experience does the company want to provide the customer?

Chapter Four: (Deliver consistently and) Go the 'extra inch'

"I'm trying to do the best I can. I'm not concerned with tomorrow, but with what goes on today." Mark Spitz
"Be faithful in small things because it is in them that your strength lies." Mother Theresa

This is the 'easy' bit. This is the 'do' that almost all books and presentations exclusively focus upon. But we know:

We won't 'do' it right
Until we 'see' it right

So now we (hopefully) see it right, we can happily and successfully focus on doing it right.

Before we start this Chapter, it's worth pointing out why the title is written as it is. The point behind it is this. It's essential to deliver your service consistently, because this is what the customer wants and what will build trust, so we have put this in brackets, as it should be taken for granted. But, as customers, we know that this is still a rare commodity, so it's essential to mention it. In fact, in many industries, if you did just this, it would be seen as going the extra inch and sometimes I start my seminars off with organisations who have, say, a 98% accuracy record by asking:

What would happen if British Airways had a 98% accuracy record on landing it's planes?

This makes the point.

Consistency is <u>essential</u> for great customer service. In fact, it's better to be consistently 'ok' than inconsistently 'great', and this fact is exploited well by many branded organisations.

But, for clarity in this Chapter, we must just focus on the second half of the title, **'Go the extra inch'**.

In order to do it right, we must do five things:

1.   Ensure the Mission is clear, Customer Focused and used as the guidance at all times for all decisions.
2.   Measure what matters in order to achieve the Mission.
3.   Act diligently and obsessively on the measures.
4.   Have a clear and obsessive scoreboard system.
5.   Have weekly 'accountability' meetings.

In simple terms:

1.   Do what matters
2.   Measure what matters
3.   Do what matters to enable us to do what matters

Good old gobbledygook: well at least you might remember it this way!

This is all called: 'Going the 'extra inch'. As previously mentioned, I use this expression intentionally, in place of 'going the extra mile' because:

- It sounds easier to do every day
- It's empowering
- Anyone in any role can do this
- It can be done at all levels, with all things
- It's the small things that make the big differences

So, in order:

1. Do What Matters

Now we have our clear CFM, and we know what the customer REALLY wants, we need to align our systems, processes and behaviours around it.

- Obsessively
- Always
- No matter what
- Even when the shareholders are shouting for us to change them
- Even when the banks are shouting for us to change them

Because, in this way and in only this way, will we prove that we are genuine and will rightfully earn the TRUST and respect of our customers and people.

Remember, no one on their death bed said:

'Well at least I made budget'

1.1. Customer Focused Leadership

There are endless books and courses on leadership, so here are some simple tips on Customer Focused Leadership.

Tip 1: Create a CFM (as covered in previous chapters)

Tip 2: Personally commit to it

Whatever your leadership role (and we're all leaders in one way or another), unless you're personally committed to the welfare of your customer because you believe it's the right thing to do no matter what, you won't succeed. Your own inner conviction is the spark that will carry you through the hard times and the lantern to show you the right decision in any circumstance.

Don't forget, your teams are looking eagerly for your mistakes. Unless you have this commitment, they'll see right through you quicker than you can state your Mission (let alone deliver it). It only takes one card to fall to bring the whole stack down.

This is VITAL.

(Note: if you find this hard - and let's face it, some MDs do - you perhaps can 'get away with' this by stating your reluctance, but employing close associates who are driven by the CFM and making sure you heed and act upon, their advice.)

Tip 3: Ensure ALL stakeholders are committed to it

This is obvious of course, but if it's not done clearly and up front, when the going gets tough the stakeholders will start to squabble and the whole thing will start to crumble.

Indeed, if the stakeholders cannot commit to the CFM, then you have to question whether or not you have the right stakeholders (and this, in itself, will be a huge leadership challenge, as we live in a dysfunctional world all too often driven by greed and short term gain).

When you explain your reasons for committing to the CFM, it is very possible that your stakeholders will not understand your motives. It is your job to educate them.

Tip 4: Invert the Triangle

As mentioned above, the 'traditional' view of organisational structure is fantastic when setting direction and communicating Vision. However, it's outmoded and disempowering as an ongoing management tool for long term success.

How many times have you heard people say, "the boss should get out more and really see what's going on"?

This quote has merit. Only by getting 'out there' is a leader going to be in a position to take on board the issues and put them right. Anyone can sit at a desk and write out policies and procedures, it often justifies their position, if only in the short term. But to make that difference and gain those precious inches, you need to get out of your office and see for yourself what's going on out there, to see how your product is being received.

An inverted triangle organisational structure will:

- Show the customer as the most important person in your organisation - not the MD!
- Show the direct customer facing personnel as the second most important
- Encourage feedback
- Get rid of pointless rivalry and sycophantism
- Allow the TRUTH to filter to the Chief Executive (which is lamentably rare otherwise)
- Focus the managers and leaders on support and empowerment

If you want empowered and committed people working for you, this is a vital step, as it's a clear visual statement of all that your organisation stands for and how it organises itself around this statement.

Tip 5: Subvert your ego to the needs of the organisation

So many leaders have become leaders through the power of their egos. Now we're telling them to leave their egos in their cars (which is why they often need such large cars to put them in), this will cause some consternation.

But it's ESSENTIAL. Pride comes before a fall and how many times have we seen this happen in practice.

The leader has two roles:

- To set direction
- To enable people to excel in the set direction

And nothing else.

Ego is a huge barrier to this. Leaders with big egos won't be able to:

- Invert the triangle
- Empower the people
- Welcome feedback

The result will be back stabbing, silo mentality, low morale and sycophantism (I've seen this too many times). Even if the people do want to delight the customer, they won't be able to, because they'll be 'too busy' doing all the other stuff. This is hard to do (we all have sensitive egos), but essential.

Because you always need to remember: **The ONLY thing that matters is the customer's needs - nothing else.**

Tip 6: Control expenditure around the CFM

This links to the above. Some of the most common indicators of an organisation in trouble are:

- Plush offices
- Directors' car parking spaces - right outside the front door
- Fountains
- Chauffeurs
- Private jets
- Team building sessions abroad

In a CFM controlled organisation, ALL activity MUST be filtered through the CFM. So, the ONLY expenditure that's permissible is that which benefits the organisation's ability to deliver the CFM. This rarely includes any of the above.

Tip 7: Focus on 'will' and 'humility'

Most people want to do a good job.

The leader's role is to ensure they stick to the CFM and support them in doing this.

Will

This is essential because it's so easy for people do get 'off track'. Just go to any meeting that's not strictly controlled around the agenda and you'll see red herrings being discussed with force and passion, while the agenda doesn't get completed in double the time allocated for it.

The leader has a huge role to ensure the organisation stays 'on track' in all they do. He or she is the only person who can do this, as they are the only one that can see the full picture.

They can only do this by constantly looking at the bigger picture, reviewing, refusing to get drawn in on the day to day decisions and trivia and obsessively focusing on the CFM as the filter for every action and every decision.

Humility

This is why it's so essential to get the ego out of the way.

Conventional wisdom would have us believe that high profile motivational leaders are the ones that get the best results. They may do for a short time.

But, in his groundbreaking book, "Good to Great", Jim Collins found through extensive research, that Companies that produced great results in the short term had what he called 'level 5 leaders'.

Here's what he means:

Level 1: Highly capable individual

Level 2: Contributing team member

Level 3: Competent manager

Level 4: Effective leader
- Catalyses commitment to and effective pursuit of a clear and compelling Vision, stimulating higher performance standards

Level 5: Executive
- Builds enduring greatness through a paradoxical blend of professional will and personal humility

He states:

"The leaders of great companies are not high profile or great celebrities. Instead, they are most likely to have come from somewhere inside the company, and will have personalities that are a paradoxical blend of personal humility and professional will. And, most often, they will contribute their success to good luck rather than personal greatness."

Further details on this can be found at: http://www.jimcollins.com

Again, this is BOCS (but so rarely common practice), as if their role is to set direction and enable others to excel in that direction, these are the two key skills needed to do this.

Many leaders mistakenly think they're there to tell everyone what to do (the Industrial Age mindset), but we know as recipients, how we behave when people do this to us. We resist. Not a very effective leadership solution.

Some examples of ways of delivering 'will' and 'humility' are:

- Setting up a transparent feedback system
- Spending time 1:1 with personnel at all levels as regularly as possible
- Managing by walking about
- Refusing to get drawn into relatively trivial issues
- Refusing to make decisions for others
- Setting values around which others can make their own decisions
- Learning from mistakes
- Helping with customer complaints and feedback

You know what you need to do.

Tip 8: Be transparent

Let's face it, there's not a lot of trust about and this is especially true between many leaders and their people. The only way to combat this is to promote transparency at every opportunity. The people may not agree with what you promote, but they'll support it and make it happen if they trust you and are convinced nothing's being hidden.

Some examples of how this can be done:

- Customer surveying (as we'll see later)
- Transparent feedback systems
- Openness with key figures
- Openness with business plans
- Openness with all salaries (are the alarm bells ringing yet?)
- One car policy for all, based on need and use, not 'status'
- Openness with Directors' perks (if any are appropriate to deliver the CFM)
- Obsessive promotion of the CFM

Tip 9: Align all systems around the CFM

Only by doing this can you enable the people to excel in the direction that's determined by the CFM. But, as a leader, you don't know how to do this, because you don't operate all the systems.

This can only get done effectively by having a clear CFM (the filter), and inverted triangle (the system to address the issues thrown up by the filter).

It all links.

Here are some examples of systems that aren't filtered by the CFM:

- Credit control systems that treat people who have had a single delay in paying in the same way as persistent late payers
- Delivery systems that don't deliver at times convenient to the customer's needs
- Personnel systems that recruit on experience rather than attitude
- Measurement systems that measure things that produce behaviour contrary to the CFM
- Marketing that treats new customers better than loyal customers

And how common are all of these?

There's lots of work to be done. But just think how fantastic you'll be if you do it.

Tip 10: Encourage feedback

There's a lot more on this later in this book, but here's a great story to illustrate the value of this tip.

In a previous life, I was involved in the motor cycle business, owning a Honda dealership. During this time, a delegation of executives from Honda Japan visited the UK to have a series of meetings in London with Honda UK.

While over here, they requested to meet with some UK dealers to gain feedback and listen to any issues they might have. I was fortunate enough to be invited to join in and following a very pleasant dinner, the table was cleared, the visitors took off their jackets and began a barrage of questions, and a whole lot of note taking.

My immediate reaction was one of "heard it, seen it all before", but how wrong I was. I would say that for every ten points of concern we raised, eight were addressed and put into action. Importantly in double quick time. Never in all my years have I contributed to such a meeting where such a response was forthcoming.

Listening to your people is one thing, acting upon the feed back is another. DO NOT give lip service.

I later worked for a large company that must have spent the same amount of money as the national debt on a staff feedback survey, "this is confidential, tell us what you really feel". Result? NAFF all! But we got the investors in people award.

Tip 11: Lead by example

Obvious again - but how often do leaders forget this?

If Nelson Mandela had not led by example during his 26 years in prison, how could he have effectively led the nation to freedom on his release?

This is very hard to do again - even the slightest trip up can have huge repercussions, but if you do, you'll inspire trust and trust is the hub of the leadership role.

Here's a great story about Gandhi, which illustrates this point perfectly:

A mother was concerned about how much sugar her son was eating and so seeking advice, she took her son to see Gandhi. She asked Gandhi if he would tell her son to stop eating sugar. Gandhi's reply was for her to come back the next week.

The following week the mother and son returned and Gandhi told the son to stop eating sugar. The mother asked Gandhi, "This was a very arduous journey for us to come to see you, why couldn't you have told my son last week to stop eating sugar?"

Gandhi replied, "Last week I was eating sugar, this week I gave it up."

This story illustrates a central tenet of Gandhi's leadership philosophy: "We must be the change we wish to see in the world." One of the reasons that Gandhi was a great leader was because he was an authentic leader. An authentic leader inspires others because they are true to their core values and purpose.

How many leaders fall at this hurdle?

- Politicians who fight 'sleaze', and then are caught fiddling expenses
- Company directors who urge cost cutting and then eat out at the best restaurants
- Managers who tell their people to manage their time well, and then ask for reports and information from their people at the last minute
- Company car policies that don't allow certain cars and then the Directors get them
- Leaders who urge restraint on pay, and then take twice the rate for themselves
- Parents who smack children and then tell them not to hit their friends

Again, absolute and complete BOCS, but rarely common practice.

To be a truly inspirational leader in any sphere of life, you HAVE to lead by example otherwise it's best not to try at all, because your people judge your actions, not your words. And they never forget.

In fact, when considering the merits of a leader through their people's eyes, there's only a very short distance between, 'a great guy' and 'a bit of a prat', and it's in this habit where that line is drawn.

I have always had a theory that we are most critical of faults in others that we see in ourselves, (consider as parents how annoying we find the children who do the things we used to do when we were their age). And, without doubt, in the absence of Customer Focused leadership, it's next to impossible to deliver great service consistently and for the long term. The Customer Focused leader is, as expected, a KEY building block to customer service success.

Do please buy and read 'Good to be Great'. It's fantastic on leadership, almost because it's not a book about leadership, but about how to make an organisation 'great' - which, of course, is what leaders are there to do. So here's a quote from Jim Collins to finish off this section.

"Enduring excellence. Great leaders not only achieve excellent results, they also succeed at a more difficult challenge: The groups they lead continue to flourish after their departure. In other words, these leaders set up their enterprises for long-term success."

That, for Collins, is the leadership litmus test. "If you had to pick one does-this-person-have-it-or-not question, that's the real test," he says. It's also the most difficult test by far, since lasting results depend on the actions of many other people and factors that are beyond the leader's control. But that's what Level 5 leaders do. They put people and the organisation in a position to succeed.

1.2. Customer Focused Strategy

Strategy means a plan, method, or series of manoeuvres or stratagems for obtaining a specific goal or result.

And an interesting note, relating to military strategy states:

"In military usage, a distinction is made between strategy and tactics. Strategy is the utilisation, during both peace and war, of all of a nation's forces, through large-scale, long-range planning and development, to ensure security or victory. Tactics deals with the use and deployment of troops in actual combat."

So this is all about plans and methods, designed over and for the long term, in order to achieve the CFM.

Too often, great missions stay as 'plans'. Typically, the energy and enthusiasm generated during the development process quickly ebbs away, swamped by the weight of day to day operational issues. The organisation and its people gravitate to fire-fighting and reactive task scheduling, instead of planning proactively to deliver the new strategic plan. The strategy is the key link between the CFM and the processes and behaviour (what actually happens).

To make the strategy 'live', everyone in the organisation needs to be engaged to take action, and organised around the key concepts of the CFM, which means:

- Communicating the strategic intent, thrusts and action plans
- Ensuring the CFM will endure no matter who is steering it
- Determining the roles and structure around the CFM, and then deciding who fits into what role
- Using rigorous project management principles based on the CFM
- Charging a fair profit from day one (not overcharging and discounting - this is hoodwinking the customer and cannot be Customer Focused)
- Discounts should only be offered for different behaviour (e.g. Increased order size, or payment by easier means)
- Increasing margins by reducing overheads and being more effective, not by clever marketing
- Increasing sales by delighting the customer, and inspiring repeat business and higher sales per transaction
- Marketing and selling focused on the customers real needs
- Turning customers into ambassadors who will bring more customers to the business
- Training people to reject the urgent and focus on the important (often erroneously called 'time management')
- Clarifying values around the CFM
- Designing systems around the customer's needs and desires to make excellent service 'routine' (especially communication systems)
- Making sure the Key Performance Indicators are aligned with the CFM and measure what the customer actually wants to be delivered
- Consistently measuring progress, assessing and giving feedback about performance in terms of what matters to the customer

There's not a lot more to say on strategy, but there's a lot to get on with here. You know what your strategy is - the customer knows what it should be. The key is to make these the same.

1.3. Customer Focused Processes (or Tactics!)

Process means a systematic series of actions directed to some end.

This is a book about customer service and not an examination of business processes, but I do think it's worth a little space to examine some key processes under the spotlight of customer service excellence.

People processes.

There are three main people processes:

1. Recruitment
2. Training and Development
3. People Management

Here are some simple tips for each one:

1.3.1. Recruitment:

If you get your CFM right and execute it excellently, it's likely that people problems will become a thing of the past, and people generally are hankering to work for the sort of organisations that do this effectively. However, if you do have to recruit, try this.

Most recruitment adverts will include the phrase 'must have experience'. My questions are, if they're good and experienced why are they looking for a job? Surely the desire to look after the customer, or a love for the particular work in question is far more important?

So, if you do need to advertise in the future, please avoid the 'must be experienced' trap (great if they are, but this should be a secondary consideration only), and go more for "People who are passionate about what they do."

There is a wonderful Hotel in Exeter, The Hotel Barcelona, where the manager does exactly this. The manager told me that the only thing she was really interested in with applicants is whether they enjoyed 'looking after people'. Beyond that, she felt her team could get them 'up to speed' on roles and responsibilities in very little time. She makes a point of meeting all applicants at second interview, and always does the first day of the induction personally. Not surprisingly, her staff turnover is way below industry average, and her 'great or poor score' (more later) is excellent, resulting in excellent profits.

A great team is your greatest business asset (how often is this stated, yet how often is it just a statement?). Recruiting a new person to your team should be done to enhance the asset.

This is how you do it:

- Be clear on the role to be filled and how it fits the CFM.

- Write a personality profile of the ideal person (use your existing people to help you).

- Use words from the personality profile with any advertising (use words like 'enthusiastic' and 'someone who enjoys working with people').

- Describe the role from the recipient's point of view, not your needs.

- Recruit and interview around the profile (involve your existing people - they need a great colleague just as much as you, and they can see all the things that you can't).

- Treat all applicants as customers. (We don't need to go into detail on this, save to say that all - successful or unsuccessful - should be treated with respect and enthusiasm. There's a very truthful saying that organisations (and people) are judged by how they treat those who have no benefit to them).

- Make every job description the same. This is crucial, and a big change to what's 'normal'. Every job is the same, i.e. to deliver the CFM. So, if the CFM is 'every customer leaves with a smile', everyone's job description is 'to create the environment where every customer leaves with a smile'. Very simple but very powerful. You can then add the roles and values afterwards. I know this works, as I've done it.

- Start the new person on a trial basis, dependent on their customer feedback score (see later).

It really is all about people; therefore it is paramount to get your recruitment and selection right first time. Yes, gut feel goes a long way, but everyone looks smart at an interview and they always say the right things. It's as if they know what question is coming next and employers always fall into the trap of thinking, they seem ok, why not?

It is essential when interviewing, that candidates are pushed so that their true character comes through. Ask them if anything funny has happened to them recently, get them to tell you a joke, tell them a joke and see their reaction. In the service industry in particular, namely catering, many positions are similar to that of an actor. They are on stage - a bar person certainly fills that role.

Here's a good story:

Some years ago I helped open up a lively young persons venue come Tapas bar. We were looking for outgoing fun staff. How could we be sure we would get the right people, staff with flair, personality, a sense of humour etc? Sitting one to one over a desk didn't seem right ,so we hired the local theatre for an afternoon. Four of us sat five rows back and invited the applicants to came on stage one at a time. We fired questions at them as they looked out into the auditorium. Yes, it was scary, but we found some great people. Some of them we could not get off the stage, they were caught up in the whole experience.

All employees reflect the people above them, so if you want to succeed and are dynamic then you need dynamic staff who will reflect your dreams. Next time you visit either a shop, pub, or restaurant and the staff are miserable and untidy, I bet you the management or owner are exactly the same. We always employ liked minded people, so if you want to be the best, employ the best.

Remember, you will never soar with Eagles if you work with Turkeys.

1.3.2. Training and development

This is so often seen as the responsibility of the HR department. It's not, it's yours. The HR department is there to help only, and the quicker that managers and individuals accept this, the better for all parties.

I had the privilege of working for a large organisation in the UK which had no HR department. While this had some issues, it freed everyone up to address the issues when they came up and knuckle down and get on with the job.

From a customer service excellence point of view, training and development should have some simple rules:

A. Training

Training is so often seen as a bit of a 'rude word'. People say they haven't 'got time' to train, or can't afford it. Often training is seen to be a solution to sort out under-performers. This is all tosh!

Can you imagine Jonny Wilkinson saying he didn't 'have time' to train, or that training should only be for the worst players in the team.

In my experience, there is a direct correlation between training and performance. And while we think about it, there is also a direct correlation between organisations' desire to measure their customer performance and the level of that performance.

All this is yet more BOCS, but worth stating anyway. Frankly, if people are your greatest asset, not training and developing them, is like not servicing your car. Daft! I would simply suggest two things.

1. Training is done in-house wherever possible (but don't try and write it all yourself, get some experts to help you, or deliver their material under licence). In this way, not only will you own and commit to it, but also you will all hold each other accountable (and this is crucial).

2. It is done according to the following priorities.

   - Vision, purpose and values (this MUST be first, but rarely is)
   - Statutory needs for the role (obviously)
   - Customer service excellence (we can help you here)
   - Other key competencies for the role
   - Ongoing development (including training people to train, coach and mentor others)

B. Development

This links in with 'people management' below, but in a nutshell, if the CFM is the most important thing in the business, then all development should focus on how to deliver this.

People development is about:

   - Training (as above)
   - Coaching and mentoring (all managers should be trained in how to do this and be confident of their ability here). Don't forget, that we are ALL managers
   - For example, a great salesperson probably holds that accolade because they are more of a coach and mentor to their customers than a sales person
   - People management (as below)

The other matter to note on 'people development' is that:

Actions speak louder than words

If you don't know what I mean by this, please read the section on 'lead by example' above.

It also means:

   - one of the best ways to develop people is to let them learn on the job, while being guided by colleagues and
   - job swaps and experience of colleagues' roles is hugely valuable in enabling people to deliver great customer service - of course!

Here's another short story:

Some years ago I worked for a company where the Chairman was once heard to ask "Why are we employing these people if we need to get them trained?"

Oh dear, a difficult one to explain. (Needless to say: this Company is no longer in business.)

The teaching profession gets this right, in that teachers are constantly offered training to enhance them in their role.

1.3.3. People management

In this section we will consider nine things:

1. Empowerment
2. Encouragement
3. People involvement
4. Performance management
5. Accountability
6. Information
7. Feedback
8. Recognition
9. What to do with the wrong people

A. Empowerment

Lesson no 1 in empowerment:

You can't empower anyone

It is frankly insulting to say to people that you will empower and motivate them.

The obvious answer from your people (with arms folded) would be: *"Go on then, let's see you try!"*

Many studies have concluded that most people possess far more initiative and ability than their job requires or allows them to deliver!

**People already have the power within them
they just need you to let them go
and help remove the obstacles**

The way to do this is relatively simple, BOCS and linked to everything else in this book:

i. Make sure the CFM is clear and empowering.

ii. Share accurate information with everyone (people without accurate information CANNOT act in an empowered way; people with it are COMPELLED internally to do it). So often organisations don't do this - and I cannot underline enough the huge importance of this. Organisations are frightened that secrets will be given away. If they are focused and aligned properly around their CFM, this will no longer be an issue. And it was tosh anyway: why treat everyone according to the lowest common denominator?

iii. Trust everyone, (links to the above) and expect trustworthy behaviour in return.

iv. Hold people accountable (for the good and the bad). Yes, people will go wrong, but mistakes are OK and can be addressed. Poor attitude isn't OK and it's this that needs addressing, very quickly and decisively, otherwise it spreads through the organisation like cancer.

v. Set very clear boundaries. Without clear boundaries, people won't know their limits, so they won't risk getting near them and thus become disempowered.

vi.   Create self-managed teams in the upside down triangle. Very simple really, people just want to 'get on with it'. They can't do this if they are not in teams with clear goals and boundaries. If you supervise people's methods you cannot hold them accountable for their results. Imagine a football game where there were no lines and the manager shouted where to kick the ball every time!

B.   Encouragement

In his book 'The One Minute Manager', author Ken Blanchard expresses this powerfully, he calls it 'catching people doing something well.'

He uses the example of the killer whales at SeaWorld in Florida and asks: "How do you get a killer whale to jump through a hoop?" The answer of course, is constant encouragement and praising progress.

The point is that you should praise PROGRESS not results. We are all learning, and if you only praise results, a few people will shine, but the vast bulk will miss out and will most likely become resentful.

To take a simile:

Imagine if a football crowd only cheered when a goal was actually scored, rather than when the ball went forwards or someone did something excellent. It would be a very boring and probably a poor scoring game!

Also, what if the team manager only praised the goal scorers at the end of the game, and not the whole team?

Yet, isn't this so often exactly what happens at work?

People crave feedback more than anything else in their jobs.

We don't need any lessons in catching people doing something badly (ask any parent), but, so often when I'm visiting organisations, people tell me how little feedback they get and how much they'd like

The usual situation is an 'assumption of good behaviour' and a focus on the bad. After all it's very easy to identify and endeavour to address issues, they're easy to see and we feel important and worthwhile if we're 'sorting a problem out'. But of course it's much harder to identify great behaviour, which is a problem, because this behaviour has so many benefits. The benefits of 'catching people doing something well' include:

a. Better motivation
b. More creativity
c. Better productivity
d. Faster learning, and of course
e. Much better customer service!

It also means that, if and when mistakes are made, if we've 'caught the person doing things well' consistently beforehand, they'll be much more likely to take criticism constructively, address the issue, learn from it, make sure it doesn't happen again and move on (rather than get offended, do the minimum to address it, learn nothing, change nothing and become resentful)!

It's not rocket science: we all want it ourselves, so why are we so bad at giving it?

Simply because of the way we've grown up:

- We start off totally dependent on others as a baby
- When we start to do things by ourselves (for example take our first step), we get huge encouragement
- This continues until about age five or so
- Then we go to school and are told to 'sit down, be quiet, and do as we're told'
- This continues until our teenage years, when we rebel (and are constantly caught doing things badly!)
- Then we realise that, in order to get a good job we need to do as we're told, and we put up with criticism
- And it continues until we become the boss and can do it to others!

I know this is a bit simplistic, but you get the picture!

So how do we give effective feedback? BOCS of course, but there are some simple rules (with thanks to Ken Blanchard), which are:

- Be specific (e.g. "the language you used when you dealt with that difficult customer was very helpful and calmed the situation")
- Pull the person aside (to show how important it is, in the same way you would if you were reprimanding them)
- Do it immediately (to get maximum impetus and benefit)
- Focus on feelings and results (e.g. "I felt very confident in your abilities when I saw you handle that difficult issue with the customer") preferably linked to the CFM
- Encourage them to do it again

While I'm sure you're all agreeing that this is a 'good idea', don't leave it there, because if you do, I can guarantee it won't happen. We just are so well programmed not to do this, that we 'forget'.

Start addressing this NOW! Create a system and rewards, to ensure these things get picked up and noticed.

For example:

- Employee of the week
- Newsletters
- Rewards
- Specific items in regular meetings

This is a hugely important aspect of creating great customer service in your organisation and needs real attention, but this is all we'll say about it for now.

For further information on this, please do have a look at 'The One Minute Manager' or 'Whale Done' by Ken Blanchard.

(Parents: this method of encouraging people to get it right works fantastically well with children – you don't have to stop at age five (and they are your customers after all!))

C. People Involvement

Very simply:

No involvement = No commitment

You can ONLY create real people commitment to delivering great customer service if you

- Involve them in strategy
- Ask them for input on crucial issues
- Tell them the purpose and reasons for decisions
- Keep them up to date with key performance indicators for the whole organisation

Many organisations try this for a short while, but get disappointed by lack of feedback and voluntary involvement from their people. Why is this? Simply because their people have never been asked with integrity before and they think it's just a phase (you'll soon get over it, you've read a book or been on a training course!). You have to show you're sincere by openly publishing things, good and bad, making them 'insiders' with key information on a systematic basis, and sticking with this. They'll come round eventually. I've seen it happen.

D. Performance Management

Performance management is normally done using three 'tools':

1. Goal and objective setting
2. Monitoring and feedback
3. Performance evaluation

The problem is that Industrial Age organisations (and I've seen this done on a premier league basis!), generally focus on item no. 3 above all others!

Each year they have a mammoth round of 'performance appraisals', where the manager appraises the employee on a mixture of objective and subjective criteria (often without having said anything to them during the whole 11 ½ months beforehand). Very often this farce results in a decision as to what salary they'll be paid in the coming 12 months. This is degrading and insulting.

Great organisations focus almost exclusively on items 1 and 2 above and if these are done properly, the need for item 3 becomes minimal. When they do carry out performance evaluation, they use a simple system and do it frequently (quarterly is widely seen as effective).

I recommend a fantastically simple form invented by Franklin Covey (www.franklincovey.com) called a 'Win/Win Agreement', or 'DR GRAC'.

It's a simple tool (see Appendix 3 for a blank copy) that enables you to do all the above by effectively agreeing (and signing that you both agree) to the following headings:

DR: stands for 'desired results'. What are the desired results of this interaction, and how do they link to the CFM?

- This is a VITAL conversation to have up front. It's about management by a clear picture of results, not by managing the process (see 'empowerment' above).

- This checks that we're aligned with the CFM.

- This paints a clear picture of the outcome needed (remember: a picture paints a thousand words), so that both parties are crystal clear on this! (How often have we given detailed instructions to people, which they've carried out to the best of their ability, only to end up with results that are totally unlike what we wanted? Just look at the 'jobs-worth' attitudes and bonkers results that detailed legislation produces!)

G: stands for 'guidelines'. There are at least two parties at this meeting and this gives the assignor and assignee the chance to discuss and agree guidelines in more detail.

R: stands for 'Resources'. Resources are people, time and money. Again, with two or more parties at the meeting, there will be many resources that can be brought to bear than only one party may be aware of originally. Discussing this in detail, enables you to get creative in this area (which is particularly vital in this era of diminishing resources and a constant demand for more results with less resources).

A: stands for 'accountability; how and when will we measure progress? Very helpful to agree this up front so we know what the 'milestones' are and when we'll be accountable for them (but how often is this spelt out up front in 'normal' situations?)

C: stands for 'consequences'. VITAL to agree up front and again, so rarely done. If this is done properly, you'll get motivation, commitment, ingredients to catch people doing something well, great career planning and a clear ability to deal with under performance. If this is not done, good performance will just be 'expected' (so no chance of catching people doing something well, and when things don't go as planned, you'll just get excuses).

All of this in order to achieve a 'win/win' solution to any issue. Fantastic!

Remember, in a healthy performance management situation, we should be practising 'servant leadership'. This means that the leader, or manager, is there to support and direct the person responsible to get the task done, and NOT to tell them how to do it!

(Note: when consulting with public bodies, one of the main issues can be their reluctance to get rid of poor performers because they are frightened of the consequences. The DR GRAC model addresses this - as well as all of the other benefits it has - as it gets both parties to sign up to consequences before the task or project is started).

E.   Accountability

In any personnel situation, the people need to know:

- What am I accountable for (what are the 'desired results and guidelines' - see above)?
- Where are the boundaries (what can I do and not do - see 'empowerment' above)?
- How does my role here link to the CFM (this is VITAL - if everyone sees how their role fits to the CFV, they'll be motivated and empowered to achieve the desired results).

Again, I repeat here what I stated above. Everyone's job description has to include a desired result that they contribute to the CFM, otherwise:

- Credit controllers will control credit (at the expense of sales)
- Personnel people will stick to regulations (at the expense of flexibility)
- Sales people will sell (at the expense of profit and service)
- Managers will manage (at the expense of motivation)

You can see what I mean.

F.   Information

In order to be motivated and empowered, people need to know:

i.   What's the score?

   a.   The player cannot be motivated and up their game when necessary, if they don't know the score. So many managers are scared that employees might give away secrets that they obscure the score. This is like ten pin bowling with a curtain across the lane (and do you think the manager would focus on the number of pins that had fallen or the number that had been missed? Yes, you guessed it - how many they'd missed).

   b.   Without a clear score a player cannot self motivate around results. With one, all players will work as a team to achieve the score.

(This is often a major issue with public bodies, where there are legions of targets and measurements, but no clear score. The result is disempowerment, lack of teamwork, and general confusion).

ii.   How are we ALL doing?

Some organisations let each department see their own figures, but won't let them in on how the whole organisation is doing (for similar reasons to above). This destroys teamwork, and creates silos. A far greater menace than any risk of information leakage. Imagine a cricket or baseball match where each player only saw their own performance figures and not the overall score!

G. Feedback

Feedback is the lifeblood of any organisation. If an organisation does not encourage it through systems and example, they will slowly strangle themselves.

We'll learn later how to gain fantastic feedback from customers, but please ensure you also glean it from colleagues (and don't think that this will happen naturally, especially in a hierarchical system - it simply won't).

Ego and fear will strangle it before it gets anywhere near the person who needs to hear it.

Likewise all colleagues need honest feedback from

- Managers
- Peers
- Subordinates

Without the fear of politics, in order to grow and develop.

The openness of intra personal feedback is a very good gauge of the real and future health of any organisation.

H. Recognition

Catch people doing something well.

I. What to do with the wrong people

At the end of the day, even if you do all the above, you'll still have some people who are square pegs in round holes.

If they stay with your organisation, you'll have a lose / lose / lose situation:

- You lose because they'll perform badly, or even be a drain on you
- The customer loses because they'll get sub-standard service
- The person will lose, because they'll be wasting their time and talents doing something they're clearly not cut out for

Don't try and get horses to fly or eagles to pull ploughs.

Use the above and your other personnel tools to liberate these people who are not doing the right role and enable them to move on to roles they'll be good at (either inside or outside your organisation) as quickly as possible.
And remember: An organisation is judged by those left behind on how well they treated those that go.

I once worked for an organisation where, due to takeovers, redundancies were not uncommon, but they were always handled swiftly and scrupulously fairly. I can honestly say that, because of this, these redundancies caused very little disruption and enabled the organisation to grow and prosper at a time when it could have been floundering.

TO SUMMARISE

Personnel development is a bit like a game of tennis. Once the coach has the right person, they need to train them, provide the right equipment, make sure the court's lines and net are clear, make sure the scoreboard is working, and then

GET OFF THE COURT AND LET THE PLAYER PLAY

By all means encourage and cheer, coach them between games and hold them accountable for the result.

BUT DON'T SHOUT AT THEM HOW TO PLAY EACH STROKE!

I wish parents at school sports understood this!

1.4. Customer Care Systems and Processes

This is where most books on customer service start!

But you now know that starting here is a bit like trying to motivate front line troops in the trenches when they don't know who or where the enemy is, or why they're at war in the first place. A bit of an uphill struggle? No wonder BOCS is so rarely common practice.

So I'm going to write very little here, apart from this:

> **All processes are customer care processes,
> because all processes affect the way we care for our customer
> in one way or another**

So they ALL have to be filtered through the needs of the CFM.

Yes, of course there are specific processes that are more focused on customer care than others (e.g. sales, after sales, returns etc). But, it's very important to understand that every part of the business contributes to the customer experience.

They are ALL customer care processes.

And if they aren't, why are they there? Are they a waste of time and resources and should they be done away with altogether?

As a general principle, there are four simple rules that should apply to every system and process. We'll call these 'the 4 golden rules of systems'. They are as follows:

A system or process MUST:

1. Be designed for the needs of the customer (filtered through the CFM)
2. Be constantly reviewed (for continuous improvement)
3. Provide added value - or don't do it
4. Allow for swift and effective addressing of issues (this is crucial as this is where the extra inch makes the real difference)

So now, let's look at an overview of some processes in a little more detail.

Sales and Marketing Processes

Sales processes: Sales is the world's second oldest profession, often confused with the first.

This is not a book about sales, but sales is an essential part of the offer to the customer, so here are some principles to ensure that your sales operation is Customer Focused.

1. Remember the CFM: you are NOT here to make money, you are here to deliver a service that is **so good that people are prepared to pay you for it**. This starts with sales!

2. Change your view from: "I need to sell as much stuff as possible to as many customers as possible", to "I need to find out each customer's needs as well as possible so I can know how best I can help them". This is a big mindset shift.

3. If the customer doesn't have a need, then you don't have a solution. If you sell to someone without a need, then you'll have a one off sale at best and a serious issue to resolve at worst.

4. Focus on the long term. (This is a major issue with sales people who often only focus on next month's figures, very often because of unrealistic targets that they have been set, focusing purely on one-off sales rather than sales linked to customer rentention). This means:

   a. Spend time up front to REALLY understand the customer's needs.

   b. Avoid the temptation to focus on your products or solutions.

   c. Listen to the customer and try to genuinely understand their needs from their 'side of the table'.

   d. Never guess at their needs or their language. Ask and clarify whenever things are not 100% clear. (Note, this will NOT make you look silly, this will make you look intelligent, as you will be showing real interest and often helping them clarify issues in their own mind at the same time).

   e. See your role as a 'coach'. You're an expert in various solutions, your role is to help the customer understand the best type of solution for their needs (and be prepared for the fact that this solution may not be one of yours).

   f. Be OK with failure to make a sale. The real failures in sales are:
      i. Failure to understand the need
      ii. Selling the wrong solution
      iii. Letting your ego do the talking
      iv. Making a 'no sale' needlessly expensive
      v. Getting no decision at all

   g. Make a win/win relationship your goal, not the sale. The sales (and referrals) will follow.

   h. If you do all the right stuff but genuinely can't get a 'win/win', go for a 'no deal'. This is where you do all the right things, maintain the relationship, add value to the customer, but agree between you that, for the moment at least, you are not going to do business for a reason you are both clear on. You will not try and manipulate the customer and the customer will not try and 'get one over' you. You have agreed to disagree agreeably! The door is still open, the relationship is strong and guess who they'll choose when they need advice on a different product, or when their existing supplier lets them down?

  i. Know the difference between 'hard' and 'soft' evidence:

    i. Hard evidence is evidence that can be quantified (e.g. "so, not having a computerised sales system is costing you £100,000 per year in lost stock?")

    ii. Soft evidence is unquantified: (e.g. "so you think your people aren't getting the best results they can?")

  j. Measure the impact of hard evidence vs. the cost of resolution. E.g. How much is it really costing you not having 'this software' compared to how much it would cost to install it, train on its usage and get it going? (This is often easier than you think and can create some amazing figures).

  k. Turn soft evidence into hard evidence through skilful questioning. e.g.

    i "Why do you think that?"
    ii "What evidence do you have?"
    iii "Who says that's the case?"
    iv "How does this show up?"
    v "How do you measure it?"
    vi "Where are the main issues?"
    vii "What would that allow you to do?"
    viii "And then what happens?"

  l. Focus on the customer, not you. 'Be there'. (This sounds easy but, in reality is very hard because we're so full of our own solutions and needs). Stimulate them to open up and keep telling you their needs, don't just listen with the intent to respond and resolve.

  m. Be wary of any prejudices you may have, (e.g.: "We see this type of thing all the time, you need to do X").

  n. When you think you've understood their needs, summarise it back to them in your own words. They'll tell you when they think you've understood them properly and then they'll be open to listen to you.

  o. Put your offer or solution into words that fit with their needs and understanding, not yours.

In a nutshell: **don't 'sell', just understand, educate and try to help people in an excellent way**.

If you do all this, you'll achieve three things:

1. Consistently great customer service
2. Lasting partnerships with customers and potential customers
3. Significantly better sales over the long term

One more thing. During the sales process, you're bound to come across what we call 'yellow lights'. These are the things that might mean the deal could turn to a 'red light'. These might come in any form:

- Misunderstandings
- Past problems
- Lack of budget
- Lack of decision making ability
- Etc

The key to Customer Focused selling is to slow down and deal with them head on through intelligent questioning, usually preceded by the phrase:

"I have a concern."

You then tell them what your concern is and ask them if they'll work with you to resolve it one way or the other (to which they almost always say 'yes'). This is opposed to the 'traditional' way of dealing with 'yellow lights', which tends to focus more on avoidance and manipulation.

Customer focused sales people NEVER do this. So, in a nutshell, to be a great salesperson you have to first of all deliver great customer service by focusing on the customer's needs and desires over and above your own. Now where have we heard that before?

(For further information on this, please read 'Let's get real, or let's not play' by Mahan Khalsa).

Marketing Processes

The best type of marketing by far, is word of mouth, but if you have to spend money on marketing, make it focused on the customer's needs (not yours).

For example:

- Aim for repeat trade more than new customers (i.e., make marketing part of your operations, not a separate issue). You do this by doing everything you've learnt in this book (indeed, if this is done well, it often negates the need for any other marketing at all - I've seen this happen many times).

- Use honest testimonials.

- Do activities that will be measurable in their effect on building your trade. Don't fall into the ego trap of brand building, unless your offer is your brand.

- Add value to your potential customer even if they don't give you business (e.g. don't have a brochure, have a 'consumers guide', which genuinely helps them understand the market better)..

- Use technology wisely (i.e. E-shots are great if they add value but a huge turnoff if they just promote you and your services).

- Consider 'tele-seminars': these are much more convenient to the customer.

- Consider the customers' future desires: e.g. localised sourcing and fair trade.

- When you find something that works, keep doing it. Don't be tempted to change because you're 'bored ' with it. It's there for the customer, not for you.

- If you offer anything for free, be honest about why you're doing it (e.g. introduction of a new product, or 'if you can see how much value I can add, you'll want to keep doing business with me').

- Offer 'above board' rewards for referrals (e.g. a donation to a charity of their choice). If you're good enough, they'll want to refer you, but this can tip them to actually do it.

- Above all make your 'brand' stand for two things:

  - TRUST and
  - making the customer's life easy

In a nutshell: **Build a reputation of trust and service first and then help people find out about you. Don't push them.**

One more thing. PRICE, the ultimate five letter word. I have just a few more things to say on price, as it relates to marketing.

a. Aim for great service first at the best price you can manage. If your service is great, price isn't nearly as much of an issue

b. If your offer is price focused, then you're probably not great at anything else

c. If you gain customers on price today, you'll lose them on price tomorrow

d. Price driven customers waste your time, pay late, steal ideas and information and complain more than other customers

Communication Processes

Communication is the essence of life.

Great customer service can only be achieved through great communication.
Great customer service cannot be achieved without great communication.

In a recent survey of recruiters from companies with more than 50,000 employees, communication skills were cited as the single most important decisive factor in choosing managers. The survey, conducted by the University of Pittsburgh's Katz Business School, points out that communication skills (including written and oral presentations) and an ability to work with others, are the main factors contributing to job success.

Consider Amazon.com: most people have never spoken to anyone from Amazon, yet, via great use of technology they :

- Offer you the products that you might be interested in because of past purchases
- Tell you where to get the best price (even if it's not with them)
- Make suggestions about other products
- Tell you what other customers have said about what you're looking at
- Thank you for your order
- Tell you when it's been sent
- Have an outstanding returns policy

How many organisations who deal with customers face to face can say that they do this?

Communication is, again, a huge subject. So as usual, I'll stick to the principles (which are of course, generally BOCS).

The main problems occurring with communication are that:

- We say something in 'organisation speak'
- Customer interprets (what they think we mean)
- Customer responds accordingly
- We interpret their response

It looks a bit like this:

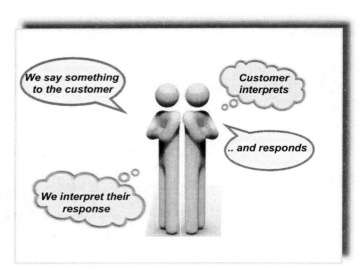

I love the story from the trenches in World War One where an order stating "send reinforcements, I'm going to advance", comes out at the other end as "send three and four pence, I'm going to a dance".

To deliver your messages effectively, you must commit to breaking down the barriers that exist in each of these stages of the communication process.

If your communication is too lengthy, disorganised, or contains errors, you can expect it to be misunderstood and misinterpreted. Use of poor verbal and body language can also confuse the message.

Don't forget, everyone's 'busy'. Be as succinct as possible - less is definitely more (please someone tell the government this!)

Once you understand this, you need to work to understand your customer's needs and desires, making sure you can converse and deliver your message to people of different backgrounds and cultures within your own organisation, in your country and abroad.

Here are some principles and ideas to help you in the main areas:

On the Telephone:

This is usually the main form of communication (apart from the dreaded email) today, so real care needs to be taken on doing it properly. Things to consider are:

- The phone number: is it easy to remember, does the customer perceive it as a cheap or expensive call to make, do we have one number for all calls, or a different number for each department?

- Direct lines: remember, a key component of customer care is that you show you care. Customers just want life to be easier by dealing with you, so direct lines to customer facing personnel are usually a good idea. Customers don't want to deal with switchboards and automated answering. They need to feel relaxed and confident that they can get a straight answer from you very quickly and the way you organise your phone system will be a key determining factor in this judgement. If it's badly organised and customers find you hard to get hold of, they can only ever be 'satisfied' with your service, and therefore will defect as soon as a viable alternative comes along.

- How many rings will it take before someone answers? (Obviously the less the better. Research shows that picking up in three rings or under indicates you're 'on the ball' and seven rings or over that you're 'half asleep').

- Who answers, in what order, in your office or department?

- How does the customer know who they're talking to and how they (the customer) can talk to the people they need?

- What happens when everyone's engaged?

- Do you have a system to manage this? (research shows that customers don't trust answer machines because people often don't return calls). So putting an answer machine in to pick up these calls will DEFINITELY lose you business in the short term, because people will just ring the next person rather than leave a message. It will DEFINITELY lose you business in the long term, because people want life to be easier, not harder, by dealing with you. Try using a phone answering service to pick up these calls.

- The customer won't know the difference and it'll pay for itself many times over. But beware, a phone answering service can only give great service to you if you tell them everyone's movements and when they'll be able to assure the customer that you'll get back to them.

- Do you have a standard greeting that portrays interest and intelligence?

- Are your front line people trained in telephone language and etiquette?

- Do all your people know about 'above the line' words?

Below the line words	Equivalent above the line words
"That's not our policy"	"That's an unusual request, I'll see what I can do to help you"
"They're not in today"	"I can't contact them today, tell me more and I'll see who else can help"
"I'll pass on a message"	"I'll make sure they phone you back by 4pm"
"If it doesn't happen please call us back"	"I'll call you tomorrow morning to make sure it's all happened. What number can I get you on?"
"You've got under a year to live"	"You've probably got 3 to 6 months of good health"
"The park closes at 8pm"	"The gates are open until 8pm"

Are all people trained and organised to take messages? I find this is often an area of huge under-performance.

Let's look at this from the customer's point of view:

You Say	Customer Hears
"I'll leave them a message"	They'll never phone me back, no one really cares about my call here, I'll try someone else
"I'll ask them to call you"	Same as above
"They're in a meeting"	No one cares
"They're not available right now, but I can see they'll be able to call you by 4pm and I'll make sure they do. What number will you be on at that time?"	Someone cares. I want to do business with these people
"Here's my direct line. If you have any further issues please ring me"	Someone cares. I want to do business with these people

Simple isn't it? Yet 90% people get this wrong. They take a 'message' and then get off their desk as quickly as possible, so they can get on with their 'work'. The problem is of perception.

The answer is to change perception to:

Everyone's 'work' is to delight the customer
and
The person who takes the message is the one responsible for getting it returned.

Good, simple, but effective stuff.

And will people actually return the call?

Another key area where people let themselves and their organisation down. I personally noticed this hugely when changing from being a Director in a large Company in the UK (where people generally phoned me back promptly), to becoming self-employed (where 90% of calls went unreturned). This is appalling. The issue is two fold:

a. Perception: People return calls according to importance. Well that's OK, but the key mistake is importance to whom? The measure of importance MUST be the CFM, not my personal ego or what might benefit me personally in the short term. Because if the ego takes over, I'll generally only return calls to people who have power over me in some way, or are a direct and immediate threat or benefit and not to others - somehow I won't quite 'get time' to return these. But we know that customer service is based on relationship and I CAN'T have a relationship with someone who doesn't phone me back, no matter how much I may want to.

b. Organisation: If I don't have a great system to organise myself I CANNOT deliver great service. Most people don't have a great personal organisation system based on what's important to a CFM, so they very often fall at this fence. If you or your people have an issue in this area, get some training very quickly **that includes a system**. Why not try 'Focus' by Franklin Covey.

From my personal experience and the consultancy work that I do, I have found that:

If organisations just get this simple thing right
they're probably in the top 10% in the customer's eyes.

This is very simple to do. It just takes a bit of time, organisation and investment.

Here's a great story that illustrates the point:

Some years ago, the brewing department of a company organised a major sales drive. The MD was not convinced that all staff were "on board" with it and cast doubt over the receptionist's ability to deal with incoming calls efficiently.

To prove his point the MD rang the brewery and pretended to be the Sales Director of a major pub company. He knew that his Sales Director was away at a meeting. So, when he got through (eventually) he asked for the Sales Director and was told, correctly, that he was away.

The MD then asked if a message could be left for him, the message being that he wanted to discuss a deal to place a firm order for five thousand barrels of beer, over a twelve month period and could the Sales Director contact him immediately on his return.

Well, to this day the message never got through. As the MD said, thank God it was not for real, but how many genuine calls like that had been made?

There's more information on personal organisation in Appendix 2.

- Does everyone use answer machines/voicemail intelligently?

Another one where there's huge issues in these days of streamlining and a constant demand for more for less. We all now have mobile phones with voicemail, the issue here is (and I can't understand why this is so hard for some people to grasp) there's no point in having an answer machine or voicemail if you don't use it properly and return those calls.

Let's look at some scenarios again from the customer's point of view:

Message States	Customer Thinks
"This is the answer machine message for 07890 123456, please leave your message after the tone."	Have I got the right number? When's he in? Is he in or away? Probably best not to leave a message?
"This is the message service for Joe Bloggs, I can't answer the phone at the moment, please leave a message and I'll call you back."	Well I've got the right person, but when will they phone me back? Today? Tomorrow? Next week? Never? I'll try someone else.
"All our lines are busy at the moment, please do leave us a message and we'll return your call promptly."	No way. I've got a life to live (unless I really trust you from past experience and relationship).
"This is the message service for Joe Bloggs, I can't answer the phone at the moment, please leave a message or try my landline on ......"	Oh bloody hell! I'll probably get an answer machine on the landline as well. Probably best to try someone else.
"Hi - you've reached Joe Bloggs on Wednesday the 9th July. I am around all day but currently unavailable. Please leave a message and I will return your call within 3 working hours. Please briefly state the purpose of your call and your phone number to enable me to reach you promptly with the right information".	Great! I'm dealing with someone who's organised and cares!
"Hi - you've reached Joe Bloggs on Wednesday the 9th July. I am in a meeting all day, please leave me a message and I'll ring you back this evening or tomorrow morning -(please let me know which would suit you best). Alternatively, if your call can't wait, please phone Bill on .... who will be able to help you or get hold of me in an emergency. Please briefly state the purpose of your call and a phone number I can call you back on, to enable me to reach you promptly with the right information."	Great! I'm dealing with someone who's organised and cares!

This is again all good BOCS, but in 90% of cases is not common practice. People use the phone because they want to sort something out quickly, or build a relationship. Not to interrupt you. Let's look at some scenarios again from the customer's point of view:

Effective use of your answering machine/voicemail is so simple to do (if you're not sure, just do it a couple of times and it'll become easy), and results in a win / win outcome if done properly:

- The customer wins because they can get issues dealt with effectively.

- You win because you:

    a. Can deal with issues much easier
    b. Manage customers expectations excellently
    c. Get sensible messages left for you
    d. Avoid irate customers if you're unavailable all day

How do we feel as a customer when we have been trying to get hold of someone, they've not changed their answer machine message and we find out, after persevering, that they're on holiday for two weeks, but 'forgot' to change their message? Not happy.

The fact that they 'forgot' tells us more than we need to know about how much they really value their customer.

Proactive Calling

A very simple, yet very important part of great customer service is what I call 'proactive calling'. This is where you make contact with your customer to deal with issues proactively.

This requires some effort on your part. You need to be well organised and consider the issue from their point of view. However, taking the time to do so will go a long way in enhancing your relationship with your customer.

(All of these principles are, of course applicable face to face and in writing).

But it ONLY works if you have the customer's best interest in mind, above all else. Here are some great examples:

- A waiter notices that someone has ordered a bottle of wine that will not go very well with the dish ordered. An alternative will complement the dish much better and will cost less. He therefore lets the customer know his thoughts in a caring and professional way.

- A manager has handled and resolved a complaint, but phones back a week later to make sure everything that should have happened has happened and tells the customer how to avoid similar issues in the future.

- A phone salesman notices that a customer is on an inefficient tariff for their usage, and tells the customer how she could get better value ... even though it may cost him some commission.

- A printing company has sent out a proof incorrectly because some communication crossed in the post, so they phone the customer to tell them to bin the proof and that another one will be in the post that night.

You can see how powerful these examples are, but, so often, they don't get done because people are 'too busy'. 'Too busy' to care - it happens all the time.

In Writing

I'll keep this short and so should you.

Customers want life to be easier by dealing with you, so they want your writing to be:

- Concise
- Clear
- Focused on their needs (not yours)

That's all.

Some of the most basic tips to remember when writing include:

- Avoid slang
- Try not to use abbreviations (unless appropriately defined)
- Steer away from symbols
- Clichés should be avoided like the plague
- Spell things correctly, especially the names of people and companies
- Quotation marks should be placed around any directly quoted speech or text and around titles of publications
- While these tips cover the most common mistakes made when writing letters, memos and reports, they in no way cover everything you need to know to ensure your written communications are accurate and understood. If you have problems in this area, get some help. Nothing detracts from your service and image more than poorly written communication.

Email

Yes, a form of writing and a fantastic communication tool, that, like everything else is often used dysfunctionally - so much so that it has now become the prime form of stress and problems in the 21st Century office.

Here are some key rules:

1. Think before you write. Just because you can send information faster than ever before, it doesn't mean that you should send it.

2. Never reply to dysfunctional email with further dysfunctional email.

3. Avoid email 'conversations'. Pick up the phone and communicate properly.

4. Remember that once it's sent it can go anywhere.

5. Keep your message concise. Remember that the view screen in most e-mail programs shows only approximately one half of a hard-copy page. Save longer messages and formal reports for attachments.

6. On the other hand, do not keep your message so short that the reader has no idea what you're talking about. Include at least a summary (action or information?) in the first paragraph of your message.

7. Tell the recipient what response you need (it's often good to do this in the subject line).

8. Don't use email for catching people doing something badly, dealing with difficult issues or disciplining them.

9. Don't "spam" your readers. Don't send them unnecessary or frivolous messages. Soon, they'll quit opening any message from you.

10. DON'T TYPE IN ALL CAPS! IT LOOKS LIKE YOU'RE YELLING AT THE READER!

11. And don't mark a message as 'important' unless it's important to the reader for their needs!

12. **Don't over-emphasise (i.e. over use of the bold function). If you emphasise everything, you emphasise nothing.**

13. Remember: there's no such thing as an 'urgent' email. If you have an 'urgent' issue to communicate, by all means send an email, but also phone to inform the recipient that your email is on its way to them. Otherwise you can't be sure that they'll see it in time.

14. Remember that what's 'urgent' or 'important' to you, may not be the same to the recipient.

15. don't type in all lower case or leave out punctuation if you violate the rules of english grammar and usage you make it difficult for the reader to read your message.

16. Use the "Subject" line to get the readers' attention. Replace vague lines ('team meeting,' or 'Sales figures') with helpful information: ('Need your input on team meeting agenda,' or 'Analysis of recent problems with sales').

17. Only copy in those who really need to know and are involved. Don't fall into the trap of including recipients that just shows you are saying "hey, look how clever I am" or "please take note boss that I'm working very hard". It's a quick way to fall out with colleagues and to become known as a creep, not to be trusted.

18.　Check email at regular intervals during the day (two or three times in most roles) but not all the time. This enables you to make better use of your time and reply to emails according to importance and effectiveness.

19.　Make sure you clean out your inbox once a day. This is a simple act of courtesy, and enables you to deliver great service.

20.　If you can't reply properly in a timely manner, send a holding email to build confidence.

21.　Always set your Out of Office agent when you are going to be away from your email for a day or more.

22.　Take the time to poof read your documnt before you send it. Even simple tipos will make you look sloppy and damage your professional crederbility!!!

Face to Face Communication

This is where your old dog can teach you some new tricks.

Most people love dogs because they're:

- Pleased to see us
- Open
- Enthusiastic

A good lesson for us when dealing with people face to face.

And we all know that cheerfulness and enthusiasm is infectious, as is miserableness and grumpiness. There is a lot of research on this subject as to why this should be, but it all basically boils down to the basic law of attraction.

We attract that which we focus upon. If we are stressed about difficult customers, we get more of them. If we deliver bad service, we tend to get bad service. If we deliver great service, we tend to get great service.

Here are some top tips:

- Be aware that 55% of all communication is body language
- Be bright and cheerful (even if you don't feel it inside, the mere act of doing it will bring you up, apart from enabling you to give great customer service - a dual benefit!)
- Focus on your facial expressions: people like happy, smiley people
- A smile is infectious
- Watch your language:
  - Avoid 'I can't', 'must', 'have to'
  - Change them to : 'what can I do', 'could' and 'choose to'
- Listen at least twice as much as you speak (we have two ears and only one mouth and these should be used in this proportion - see below)
- Speak clearly and succinctly
- Deal with issues directly, don't try and gloss them over
- Use physical contact as much as possible (where appropriate to your situation, audience and location)
  - Handshakes
  - Kiss
  - Pats on shoulder
  - Etc
- Show real interest in them for their own sake: they are a human being just as important as you, with needs and desires. If you're not genuinely interested in them, they're very unlikely to be interested in you
- Use eye contact
- Make sure you have good personal appearance

Listening Skills

This applies to all the above situations and is a skill most of us are sorely lacking in.

Why is this? Well, we've been taught endlessly to read, write and speak both in and out of school, but we've never been taught to listen properly - it's just assumed that we will. However, it's a very difficult skill, but hugely important to get right. This is because people just want you to care and value them, and listening well is the best way to do this.

Here's how you do it.

People speak at 100 to 175 words per minute, but they can listen intelligently at up to 300 words per minute. Since only a part of our mind is paying attention, it is easy to go into mind drift - thinking about other things while listening to someone. The cure for this is active listening.

Here are some tips:

- Put yourself in a compassionate and interested mindset (if you don't do this, you can't do all the rest of this stuff). You want an outcome that's a 'win/win'. This means that both parties need to come away from the interaction better off than they went in.
  - Unfortunately our ego usually drives us only to consider a 'win' for us. This results in two one-way conversations where neither party really listens to the other because they're too busy considering their own needs.

- Once you've identified and addressed a win for the other person, they'll want to identify and address yours. Unfortunately, this rarely happens, because none of us have been taught to listen properly, so you must assume that you'll need to take the lead on this and listen to them first.

  - **With the intent to understand them from their point of view.**

• Remember, the key to success is to **deliver a service that is so good that people are prepared to pay you for it**. You can't do this unless you understand the other person first.

• Make sure the environment is conducive to proper listening (no interruptions, background noise etc if possible).

• Be silent. Show the other person that you want to listen to them: Use a lot of eye contact, nod, ask open questions, show empathy.

• Check compliance. Use phrases like, "I need to listen to you in order to understand you fully, is that OK?"

• If you need to take notes, make sure they're shorthand or key words only. Try to maintain as much eye contact as possible. (And again, it helps to check compliance).

• Be patient. Don't reply, advise, probe, interpret, judge, evaluate etc. They will let you know when they are ready to listen to you.

• Watch your own emotions and ego. When the other person is saying something that connects with these, there is a huge inner drive to jump in. If you do this, you'll miss what they're trying to say, and instead see it though your own emotions and experiences. This is a hugely common issue. You have to be able to stand apart from your needs and desires and simply dispassionately want to understand the other person's.

• Be slow to disagree and argue. This is not a question of 'right' or 'wrong', it's simply a question of understanding (and this is a lesson all families need to hold dear). You cannot get to a mutually acceptable outcome (a 'win/win') if you're arguing. You'll get a compromise at best, but usually something much worse.

• Ask lots of questions. <u>Never assume you know what they're trying to say, and never guess</u>. Ask the speaker to explain things. Doing this will not make you look foolish, in fact it will have two benefits:

  - firstly it will help the speaker gain clarity in their thinking (with you being a coach),
  - secondly it will add to your own understanding of the situation.

• You will know when you've truly understood them, when you can repeat back to them what they're saying in your own words and they say 'that's exactly what I mean'. When you're at this level, you're both communicating excellently.

• Keep checking compliance, with phrases like 'can we keep discussing this until we can reach a solution that we're BOTH happy with'.

In general

- Listen at least twice as much as you speak (two ears, one mouth!).

Here's a simple test for you to score your ability in this crucial area:

Score yourself on these statements, from 1 (strongly disagree) to 5 (strongly agree):

Statement	Score
When interacting with someone I tend to talk more than I listen	
I often interrupt people	
I often don't remember what someone has just said to me	
When listening, I often focus on what I'm going to say next	
I often judge people as either 'worth listening to' or 'not listening to' before they've started speaking	
I often find myself reacting emotionally to one thing that someone has said whilst ignoring the other points being made	
I am good at pretending to listen to others while thinking about something else	
I can't understand why people don't listen to what I'm saying more	

What's your score?

8 – 16 : you find it easy to be a good listener
16 – 24 : you need to brush up some skills
24+: you need to pay real attention to this!

Body Language

All the above must be filtered through the lens of great awareness of body language.

In all communication, the vast majority is through body language. Here's a diagram to illustrate this:

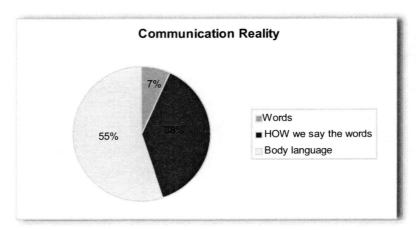

So what is 'body language' and how do we deal with it?

In simple terms, body language is the subconscious communication we give out by our appearance, expressions, and tone. Again, it's a huge subject on itself and stems from a very simple principle:

We attract what we give out.

So here are some tips on key areas of body language.

- Facial expressions: keep them positive, even if you don't feel like this inside.

- Appearance: be smart and tidy (have you noticed how great workmen generally have neat toolboxes and leave sites clear and free of mess?).

- How we sound: are you sounding enthusiastic or in need of stimulation?

- Words: are they 'above the line' or 'below the line'.

- Emphasis: on what words? The emphasis changes the meaning entirely. Try to focus on what's important to the customer.

- Ways of talking: use of pauses, speed of speech, tone of voice.

- Posture: poor posture makes you feel bad (just try changing you posture now to a more 'positive' one. How does it change the way you're feeling?). Maintain a positive posture as much as possible and this will help you maintain a positive attitude.

- Head movements: nodding shows interest.

- Hand movements: folded arms indicate defensiveness, open gestures indicate a willingness to understand and help.

- Eye movements: eye contact indicates interest. Raising your eyes indicates boredom. Winking tells the other person you're interested in them or sharing a secret.

- Body contact: despite governmental interference, people like body contact: a hand shake or a pat on the back is supportive and encouraging.

- Closeness: be very aware of other people's private 'space'. This can be different for different people and for different cultures. But there is nothing more off-putting to a customer than you invading their 'space'.

And remember, on the phone, body language is communicated through tone, volume, pitch, inflection and courtesy.

Communication Roundup

To round this section up, please put yourself in the mindset of your customer. Consider their needs, and answer these questions:

- What problems might they have in understanding the services you provide? (It may be clear to you, but is it communicated in the words and needs of the customer?)

- Do you give off body language that indicates you're there to help the customer?

- What about the other people in your organisation?

- What about your premises?

- What about your processes / contracts / documents?

- What materials need to be clearer? Better defined? Easier to get?

- What does your website communicate to someone who doesn't know you?

- Do your hours and working practices fit the customer's need?

- How easy is it to contact you personally? How do you manage email and phones?

- And how about all the other people in your organisation?

- Are you well organised to return calls?

- Are your colleagues well organised to return calls?

- Does your marketing material give a clear and consistent message?

- Are your systems designed to treat the customer as someone of value (i.e. ready access to name and relationship history) rather than just a number? (This is increasingly important in this age of remote working and there are some excellent systems out there to help you do this).

- Do you have ready access to helpful information for your customers with ancillary services they may need?

"A dog is not considered a good dog because he is a good barker. A man is not considered a good man because he is a good talker."- Buddha

Production Processes

As a producer, you'll know your production processes better than anyone and especially better than your customer. The key thing is to focus on and anticipate the customer's needs.

You need to know where the potential bottlenecks are, both now, and in the future. (It always amazed me that beer companies used to take holidays at Christmas) and with all your processes:

Begin with the end in mind

The 'end in mind' is basically to ensure that your customer gets everything on time in full.

They only want their life to be easier by dealing with you. They're not interested in how you do it - they just want you to do it. And if you don't for any unavoidable reason, you need to ensure there is a Customer Focused contingency and communication plan to deal with this.

Remember, any chain is only as good as its weakest link.

Supplier Processes

Simply.

- Ensure you treat your suppliers like you treat your customers (this is a lesson that supermarkets are learning to their cost).

- Ensure your suppliers work with you as a partner in your 'chain' to deliver your CFM. They need to know and support your CFM, so they understand your motivation.

- Measure and appraise them on their contribution to your CFM.

- Ensure you have a backup if a supplier becomes a 'weak link'.

Other Processes

Ensure all processes are filtered through the CFM. Remember how much a new customer costs vs. retaining and delighting an existing one. Consider the following to 'wow' the customer:

Making your service level transparent or guaranteed. e.g.
- 'We deliver on time or you don't pay for delivery'
- 'Your lunch will be on your table within five minutes of your order or it's on us!'
- 'If we get it wrong, you get it free'

Simple, Customer Focused guarantees. e.g.
- Consumer goods: *'If you're not satisfied at any time, you receive your money back'.*
- Service provider: *'The last thing you need is extra cost, if we haven't added value to you, we don't expect you to pay'.*
- Manufacturer: *'It does exactly as it says on the tin or your money back'.*

Many organisations are very worried about guarantees ('What if people take advantage of us?'). Yes, 1 or 2% of small minded people will take advantage (who didn't try sending a Mars Bar back to the factory when they were a kid?), but 99% of people won't. They'll see this as a genuine desire to build trust. The 1 or 2% is the cost of the guarantee. These same organisations will happily plough huge amounts of money into sales and marketing, whilst thinking that a guarantee will be too costly.

A guarantee has a second major benefit. It makes you pull your own finger out to ensure your processes work.

The desire, or otherwise, to give a transparent guarantee is one of the simplest tests of an organisation's genuine desire to deliver great customer service - or not.

1.5. Handling Complaints

The first thing to ask about customer complaints is, **why is the customer complaining?** There can only be two reasons:

- Either something has gone wrong with your service (or the customer's expectation of your service)
- Or your service is fine but something's wrong with them

Either way a complaint is a great opportunity to excel and definitely not a threat to your ego!

Taking the two scenarios above, here's why it's a great opportunity to excel.

- Scenario One: They've complained because something has gone wrong with your service. In this case, the complaint can be seen as a compliment because:

  a. It's something you need to know about for future excellence
  b. The customer is showing that they trust you enough to share something that's upset them, with you
  c. The customer wants to resolve this amicably with you
  d. If you do the above and exceed the customer's expectations, it's quite likely they'll become a fan of yours

- Scenario Two: Your service is fine but something's wrong with them. In this case, they're probably a 'difficult customer' (see below), but it's a great opportunity for you to excel because:

  a. If you handle it well they'll be grateful to you
  b. They might be telling you something really useful that no one else has noticed because they have thicker skins

In fact, there's no reason to treat complaints as any different to the basics of communication.

The way to communicate with someone when they're feeling upset or aggrieved is the same way you'd communicate with them when they're not.

With respect, compassion and a true desire to understand them, and firmness in our conviction that we're trying to give a great service and are not a bunch of numpties.

1. First, put yourself in the mindset to listen with the intent to understand ONLY. Not to judge or resolve, just to listen (see 'listening skills' above).
2. Thank the person for taking the time to tell you about the problem.
3. Listen, only asking questions to clarify.
4. Establish all the facts, whilst empathising with their feelings.
5. Once you've done this, they'll want to listen to and work with you to resolve the issues.
6. Agree specific, clear, time-bound resolutions (not vague assurances, which mean you don't really care).
7. Make sure you carry out those resolutions, and then go the extra inch.
8. Follow up (you'll find this is the extra inch). If you follow up on complaints (usually by phone), you'll really blow them away, because most people don't. They just assume everything will be OK.

And remember the facts on complaints:

95% of people don't bother to complain
They just go elsewhere and tell all their friends instead

So, what are you going to do? Get upset and let your ego destroy your service, or treat the complainant like a fellow human being with needs and desires, that you are in the perfect position to fulfil?

Of course, looking at it this way:

a complaint is a huge compliment

But remember: make sure to tell everyone else in your department or organisation, because we all know that any chain is only as good as it's weakest link.

1.6. Handling Difficult Customers

So now we know about how to handle genuine complaints, how do we handle fake ones?

Unfortunately, many people have such ego issues, that they can't tell the difference and so many complaints are handled by perceiving the complainant as a 'difficult person'.

Even worse, many organisations design their whole complaints system around the desire to stop difficult customers getting 'one over' them. So they treat all complainants by the lowest common denominator. Just like some hotels do by taking your credit card details when you check in.

So how do we know when someone is just being 'difficult'? Generally, we don't, but we find out by treating the issue:

- With respect, compassion, a true desire to understand them and firmness in our conviction that we're trying to give a great service and are not a bunch of numpties. (i.e. In the same way as with complaints).

So when we know someone is just being 'difficult', what do we do?

We continue with respect, compassion and a true desire to understand them, but we shift the balance from trying to understand the complaint (which is now a smokescreen), to trying to understand the person and most importantly. WHY they're being difficult.

In doing so, we strengthen our conviction in our own abilities and excellence of service, because if we can get at the nub of the issue, we'll probably get a raving fan and a business ally. We may again find out other information about our business, or in many instances, a rival's business.

A mindset change is often needed from 'they're a nightmare, making my life difficult' to 'they're a troubled person, making their own life difficult'. The thing is that difficult people are difficult wherever they are - it's not you, it's them.

And they have to live with it 24 hours a day, 365 days a year. They go around being difficult with everyone and they get difficult responses from everyone. We all know people like this, and we've all experienced this (isn't it amazing how all the slow drivers suddenly appear on the roads when you're in a tearing hurry?) and it's not generally a happy experience. So compassion and empathy is the key need.

If you do this, follow all the steps as for complaints and most essentially, stick to the facts and avoid the emotions, ensuring all around you do the same, I can guarantee you'll resolve 80% of 'difficult' customers' issues. The joy is that, when you do this, those people will become your most loyal advocates, because you're the only one that treats them nicely - everyone else treats them as a pain in the neck.

I know this from personal experience running pubs. It has happened many, many times.

But there will always be the few who you just can't get through to - you can't please all the people all the time. With these people, the only course of action left, when you've exhausted all the above, is to go for 'no deal'. Be firm on the facts that you can't help them, NEVER get involved with emotions and name calling, tell them you'd be delighted to help them in future situations if certain issues change and ensure they leave your business with as little upset or damage to the other 'good' customers. It's called 'agreeing to disagree agreeably'!

Here's an amazing story about difficult customers:

"I guess I didn't handle it by the 'book' and looking back part of me is not proud, but when I think about it now, it was very satisfying. I was manning the hostess point in a very busy steak bar, it was extremely busy and I was taking bookings from people and asking them to take a seat in the bar and that I would call them to come through when their table became available.

Then up he comes, "I want a table for two now". I explained we were currently full but if he and his wife would like to go the bar for a drink I would let them know when a table was available in about thirty minutes if that was alright.

He then spotted a table for four with two people sat on it. "Put us on that one, there are two spare seats." "Sorry sir, I can't do that, it would be an invasion of their privacy and for all I know it could be an anniversary they are celebrating".

He then said: "Go and ask them if they mind." I replied, "No sorry Sir, I am sure out of politeness they would agree to you joining them, but deep down it could spoil their evening".

He kept on and on, so I then explained to him quite clearly, " Sir, if I were them, you would be the last person I'd want to share my table with, do I make myself clear ?"

Funny, but he turned around got hold of his wife and left. Several customers in the vicinity burst out laughing and thought it wonderful, so I actually pleased more than I upset.

There are of course some things you can do to avoid 'difficult' customers in the first place. These include:

- Designing all your systems, processes and behaviour mechanisms around your CFM (of course)
- Being honest as to what customers you can't help (you can't be all things to all people, so don't try.   Do a few things well, rather than lots of things averagely)
    - An example of this done well: Ebay: just do one thing
    - An example of this done badly: The 5* restaurant that also has a pool table and satellite TV
- Managing expectations so you don't mislead people (guided by the above principles)

Complaints and difficult customers. If you find the above a bit hard to swallow (and many do): here's a great quote from the richest man in the world at the time of writing (so he must know one or two tricks).

"Your most unhappy customers are your greatest source of learning." - Bill Gates.

Managing Expectations

1.7.   Acres of Diamonds

This is a great story that's been told around the world. This one is from www.nightingale.com

The story - a true one - is told of an African farmer who heard tales about other farmers who had made millions by discovering diamond mines. These tales so excited the farmer that he could hardly wait to sell his farm and go prospecting for diamonds himself. He sold the farm and spent the rest of his life wandering the African Continent searching unsuccessfully for the gleaming gems that brought such high prices on the markets of the world. Finally, worn out and in a fit of despondency, he threw himself into a river and drowned.

Meanwhile, the man who had bought his farm happened to be crossing the small stream on the property one day, when suddenly there was a bright flash of blue and red light from the stream bottom. He bent down and picked up a stone. It was a good-sized stone, and admiring it, he brought it home and put it on his fireplace mantel as an interesting curiosity.

Several weeks later a visitor picked up the stone, looked closely at it, hefted it in his hand, and nearly fainted. He asked the farmer if he knew what he'd found. When the farmer said, no, that he thought it was a piece of crystal, the visitor told him he had found one of the largest diamonds ever discovered. The farmer had trouble believing that. He told the man that his creek was full of such stones, not all as large as the one on the mantel, but sprinkled generously throughout the creek bottom.

The farm the first farmer had sold, so that he might find a diamond mine, turned out to be one of the most productive diamond mines on the entire African Continent. The first farmer had owned, free and clear acres of diamonds. But he had sold them for practically nothing, in order to look for them elsewhere. The moral is clear. If the first farmer had only taken the time to study and prepare himself to learn what diamonds looked like in their rough state, and to thoroughly explore the property he had before looking elsewhere, all of his wildest dreams would have come true.

The thing about this story that has so profoundly affected millions of people, is the idea that each of us is at this very moment, standing in the middle of our own acres of diamonds. If we only had the wisdom and patience to intelligently and effectively explore the work in which we're now engaged, to explore ourselves, we would most likely find the riches we seek, whether they be financial or intangible or both.

Before you go running off to what you think are greener pastures, make sure that your own is not just as green or perhaps even greener. It has been said that if the other guy's pasture appears to be greener than ours, it's quite possible that it's getting better care. Besides, while you're looking at other pastures, other people are looking at yours.

The point of this story in this context is simple.

Get your processes right to gather your acre of diamonds from your existing customers before you spend fortunes on seeking out diamonds elsewhere (in new customers).

1.8. Checks and Balances

Simply: build in processes, checks, reviews, measurements and audits, to make sure this all happens. The best one is the customer feedback system that we'll look at later.

There's not a lot more to say on processes, but there's a lot to get on with here. You know what your processes are - the customer knows what they feel like.

The key is to make them feel like they would if you managed to deliver your CFM.

2. Measure What Matters

This is the subject of Chapter 2 of Section 3.

3. Do What Matters to Enable Us to Do What Matters

Once we have our excellent and workable measure of how we're delivering our CFM, we need to slightly alter the well-known serenity prayer.

Lord
Give me the courage
To change what I can change
The perseverance
To stick with it no matter what
The integrity
To help my colleagues do the same
And the wisdom
To listen to my customers

We can't change everything and we can't get everything right every time. But we can have the courage to honestly and genuinely listen to what our customers tell us (through our forthcoming excellent feedback system) and the integrity to grow and develop our behaviour, and that of the others around us, to meet his or her needs.

When we do measure and listen to our customers, this is not the end of the matter. We have to:

TAKE ACTION

To make sure that the feedback being given to us is used wholeheartedly in improving the service that we give.

In order to do this we need three things.

1. A clear and obsessive scoreboard
2. Weekly accountability meetings
3. Actions and policies aligned to scores

There is more about this in Section 3, Chapter 2. But briefly and in turn:

3.1. A clear and obsessive scoreboard

If you are measuring, you must have a scoreboard, otherwise there's little point in measuring.

The scoreboard must be:

- Prominently sited (so all can see it every day)
- Shown as a team effort (not individual)
- Continually updated (otherwise it just becomes part of the furniture)
- Linked clearly to the CFM (so people can see how it joins up)
- Have ideas and comments, good and bad, from your customer

Then people will take notice of it.

When they do take notice of it, they in turn will need to devise their own measures, by role / group or department, that if they deliver them, will result in the main organisational scoreboard moving forward.

I am not going to write a lot on this because it seems so obvious, but our experience shows that this rarely happens and one of the most common issues we encounter in organisations, is that the people often feel they are working 'in the dark'.

This is the most effective lead measure you can have. Be obsessive about it and use it well.

(This is often an area where organisations may need help: please contact us if you'd like our further advice in this area).

3.2. Weekly Accountability Meetings

One of the most common criticisms of training is that 'it sounds good, but nothing changes afterwards'.

This is so often true.

Very simply, in order to **get different results, you have to do different things**. The key different thing to do, when you have the world's most powerful lead measure, is to meet regularly to create a rhythm of improvement throughout your group/department or organisation. This will enable this group to 'go the extra' inch every week.

This is how you do it:

Once the key scores are measured and published weekly, all teams should have a weekly meeting to:

- Learn how their own department score contributed to the overall score
- Agree how they're going to 'move the scores forward' this week, on an individual basis

The meeting should be no more than 15 to 20 minutes (no AOBs or chit chat), of focused and targeted review and action planning.

Proposed agenda:

1. Overall score (2 mins)
2. Our score and how it contributed (2 mins)
3. Individual input (2 minutes per person timed with a stopwatch)
   i. One thing that was excellent last week, and what we can learn from it
   ii. One thing that was not so good last week and what we can learn from it
   iii. Review of last week's personal commitment to do one thing to improve the score
   iv. One personal commitment on what I personally can do to improve the score this week
   v. What support I need to do this
4. End on a high with a thanks / reward / catching someone who did something excellent last week. (1 minute).

As you can see, timing is critical, otherwise this'll become a drag. So each meeting will need a person with a stopwatch strictly monitoring the timings and keeping the participants to it. Manager's preparation is, as ever, essential.

As previously stated, if you only do one thing from reading this book, start measuring, because this is the catalyst that starts everything else moving. I would now state:

If you only do two things, start measuring, and start having weekly accountability meetings.

3.3.   Actions and policies aligned to scores

The real test of this material and the value our organisation places on the score will be determined by how all this activity affects future policy, decisions and rewards. We'll need to ask:

- Does it affect my performance as an individual?
- Does it influence and change policy and procedure?
- Does it influence future strategy?
- Do the senior management and other stakeholders treat it as 'the holy grail'?

Or is it just a flavour of the month?

BOCS of course as to which behaviour will produce what outcome. But this is rarely BNCP. That's why so few organisations excel in the long term.

We have covered many behavioural issues at length in this chapter. The only thing that we need to end with, is the strong belief that we can always improve and change and we never know better than our customers.

**The customer is not always right
but they are always the customer!**

In the immortal words of Bertie Wooster: *'Jeeves, do you know everything?'*

Jeeves: *'I really don't know sir'.*

SECTION THREE

Chapter One: Tools and Tips

This chapter is a round up of helpful information that I haven't mentioned in the previous chapters. It is a mixture of resources and tips that I've learned from others as well as from personal experience (good and bad). So here goes.

Let's start with a quote that I enjoy, and may or may not add some value to this chapter!

"He who is in love with himself has at least one advantage – he won't encounter many rivals in his love." - George Lichtenberg, 18th Century Scientist.

1. Websites and Brochures

Websites and brochures are only methods of communication like anything else, and should follow all the same rules as above.

Remember: the customer just wants two things, TRUST and for their lives to be easier.

Trust

You can make your material trustworthy by:

- Making your offer and price transparent
- Making honest testimonials available
- Focusing your offer and wording on the customer's needs and desires (not your product)
- Giving as much free information on your service as possible, so they can make an informed decision on the service or product you offer
- Providing contact details (preferably an address and land line)
- Making personal guarantees clearly available
- Making it clear if you have service delays or problems

Making Lives Easier

You can make your customer's life easier by:

- Keeping it short and simple (we all have too much info, don't add to it)
- Building trust as above
- Making it fun, relevant and interesting
- Making personal contact easy

For two really good examples of these, see Amazon or Ebay.

Unfortunately, many websites and brochures get carried away on a wave of byte sized info euphoria, so they dazzle and confuse you, rather than giving you the information you actually want!

Remember: Your website or brochure is just a tool to help you deliver your service - NOT an entity in itself.

Don't let the I.T. people design your site - let the designers do that (and probably better, your own common sense), then let the I.T. people make it work. Do keep testing from the customer's view and make feedback easy.

(For more website tips, see Appendix 5).

2.   Contact Technology

The other great scourge of the 21st Century, as it's so easy to contact lots of people quickly, everyone does it! Net result: no one reads or reacts to anything they're not directly interested in.

Lose / Lose.

This great dysfunction can be addressed if you have the integrity and patience to do things differently. As with all customer service, it's all about creating trustworthy relationships and contact technology is no different. Use it to add value, in simple, regular bite sized chunks (and remember, this is about adding value to your customer in their eyes, for their needs, not yours). This can be done though:

- Email marketing
- Tele-seminars
- Recorded messages
- Webinars
- Etc

The point of all of these must just be to build value and trust.

The thinking is, if you prove you're a 'good egg', the customer will start listening to you and when they do need a product or service that you offer, they'll probably consider you first. It really is as simple as that.

Beware: lots of marketing companies will want to take more and more money off you in this area, but you're going to be more and more in the driving seat. Because. with improved technology, most of these types of activity will be able to be measured for the impact they create. This will empower you as a customer of them in the same way that your customers will be empowered as customers of you.

This is a huge hot potato for the future.

3.   The other type of contact technology

"While you hold, we'd like to tell you about our recent award for the most confusing answering system in Europe..."

These have been discussed above, and they follow the same rules, but here's a story that happened to me as I was writing this passage!

I was trying to get a new credit card for a long trip abroad (some credit cards are better on this than others), and got a phone number off the Internet. This took me to a voice activated reception machine. I chose the option that directed me to 'credit cards', and then to 'new applications'. So far so good, but when the phone was picked up by a human, they told me I had got through to the wrong department! They then threw me directly back into the voice activated nightmare (which did recognise some of the words I used and so cut me off!). I tried again, with exactly the same result.

So I looked for a different number and got through to a 'customer service' department (what kind of activity were all the others doing, I wondered). I asked the very helpful representative to help me by resolving my issue. They then told me that the wait was at least 5 weeks (despite the website telling me it was 5 days), so I finished by asking them how much they spent on advertising their rotten cards and whether perhaps some of that money could have been better employed making their service actually work.

An amazing fact - when you're kept waiting on line by an annoying machine that plays dreadful piped music at you (or, even worse tells you how great the company you're wasting your life waiting for is), the message is always:

> "We're experiencing an unusually high number of calls at the moment."

> And never (which would be more truthful and therefore build a bit of trust).

> "We're a bit short on numbers in the office at the moment / we've made a bit of a cock-up, we're really sorry to keep you waiting."

Even the machines consider the organisation's needs on top of the customers! I guess: 'in times like these it helps to recall there have always been times like these!'

4.   Mystery Shoppers

These are a great resource and can provide valuable feedback on specific issues, but please note this: they cannot be used to measure customer service! Why not? Because they are subjective and only cover single transactions. Any results can and are widely disputed by managers, so the whole exercise can become pointless or even harmful.

The only way they could provide helpful customer service information would make using them uneconomic. By all means keep using them to test systems and measure specific issues, but don't use them to measure your general levels of service.

You already have an expert in this area, and they'll tell you for nothing!

5. Appropriate Marketing

Marketing only works if it fulfils the customer's needs, so the closer you can anticipate and then fulfil those needs, the more effective your marketing will be. For example, Amazon sends you suggestions based upon past purchases. On the other hand Vista Print tends to bombard you with offers and confusing deals, which can actually destroy trust and confuse the customer!

Here are the customer's needs that you need to fulfil by category.

1. **Potential customers:** they need to understand your offer, and why they should trust you, in order that they make a sale.

2. **Existing customers**: they need to build trust and partnership with you in order to trade up. You need to focus on making their life easier and finding out what will 'wow' them to build the trust.

3. **Great customers**: they want to recommend you, so you need to do all the above, go the extra inch, and make referring you easy. They will only refer you if they fully trust you.

6. Hospitality

From the point of view of customer service, this can be a double-edged sword. For some people, good hospitality will build the relationship, for others it can ruin it. The key is to understand your customer's needs, and keep all hospitality appropriate.

For example:

- Customers who are a bit insecure might consider lavish hospitality as a gesture of friendship and this might build the relationship (but, beware, this will be a relationship that will crumble just as easily).

- Customers who are thrifty with their money, might regard any hospitality as a waste of money that would be better spent keeping your prices down.

A sensible rule of guidance would be:

- If the hospitality adds real value to the relationship (not false value) for it's own sake, and contributes to better business understanding or practice for the customer, then it'll probably be a builder of trust and therefore enhance the customer relationship.

- If it doesn't, then question why you're doing it. If it doesn't fit through the CFM filter, cut it.

7.   Added Value Schemes

With these, all that you need to remember is how much it costs to get a new customer versus retaining an existing one. These are split into two areas:

- Firstly: 'loyalty' schemes: you see these in every supermarket. They are a simple and effective way to show your loyal customers that you value them, and to give them a little bit back. The more business they give you, the better they get rewarded. Whilst these do build relationships, they are icing on the cake, rather than a part of the cake itself. The most important thing a business can do for it's customers is to make their life easier and build trust with them. If they don't do this, a loyalty card won't save them.

- Secondly: ensuring that existing customers get access to the same deals as new customers. This is one that FDs and marketing people hate, but let's look at it from the customer's point of view.

    - How do I, as a customer, feel when my bank gives a new customer a better deal than the one I'm on when I've been with them for 20 years?

    - How do I feel when a mobile phone agent offers new customers significantly better deals than I can get on renewal?

Of course, the answer is – FED UP!

So, as a customer I'll join in the dysfunctional behaviour and change suppliers frequently, to keep up with the good deals.

This must cost organisations BILLIONS every year, not to mention the time and effort wasted by the customers! Isn't it time for a change?

8.   Premium Customers

As part of the mindset change, we can start to focus more upon, and treat differently, our 'premium' customers.

Remember the 80/20 rule: 80% of the results come from 20% of the activities

And it's the same with customers: as a general rule, the majority of profits will come from a small minority of customers (and, conversely, the majority of problems and issues will come from a minority of customers at the other end).

So, the question we need to ask ourselves, is how we treat these people particularly well without annoying and upsetting our other customers?

The best thing to do is always to consider what principles apply to the situation. The key principle with customer service is always 'treat your customer as you would wish to be treated if you were them'. So, as a premier customer, I may wish to be treated by:

- Having minimum order levels waived
- Having a personal manager
- Be invited to previews or special events
- Being asked for my opinion or input to new products or services
- Being invited to join a special club or group

And all of these can be done professionally and functionally, without upsetting other existing customers. In fact, premium customers will often pay more to be treated in this way and non premium customers will often aspire to this level of service and therefore increase the business that they do with your organisation.

9. Keeping Track of the Competition

No matter how good you are, or think you are, it's always a good idea to keep track of what potential competitors are doing. Of course, the best way to do this is to be a customer of theirs yourself, but this is not always possible. Therefore, this is a good place to involve all members of your staff (perhaps mystery customers), but this will only happen if you set up a system and monitor it regularly and properly.

The best system is the one we advocate in the next chapter, because, although you don't like it much, your customers are also the customers of your competition. When you listen to them properly and act on the information they tell you, you can not only find out what your competition are great at, but also adapt quicker to the customer's future needs.

In my experience, this vital activity is usually done in an 'ad hoc' and disorganised fashion, if at all. On top of this, very often the ego takes over and all benefit and learning is lost in an orgy of criticism and nit-picking of your competition.

The great organisations keep a very close eye on the competitors, listen and learn from them, accept that they all have something to learn from each other and that no one gets it right all the time. The winners are the ones who adapt quickest to the needs and desires of the customer.

As Charles Darwin said:

> *"It is not the strongest of the species, nor the most intelligent, that survives. It is the one that is the most adaptable to change."*

> *"In the long history of humankind those who learned to collaborate and improvise most effectively have prevailed."*

> *"Ignorance more frequently begets confidence than does knowledge."*

I think that makes the point well.

10. Measuring Success

Here's the 64 million dollar question. How do we accurately and effectively measure all this?

Because: What gets measured gets done

and

If you can measure it, you can move it.

All organisations have measures. Indeed, organisations usually have measures ad nauseam. This is particularly a problem with public service organisations that tend to have many stakeholders with different needs and desires, and therefore far too many measures which are often not complimentary and sometimes even contradict each other.

The problem is twofold:

- Firstly: most organisations have **too much data and not enough information**. This is just getting worse and worse with mankind's ability to measure more and more things. Confusion is often king.

- Secondly: most measures only tell us what has happened in the past (these are called lag measures).

So we need a key measure that will aid us in delivering outstanding customer service. This measure must be simple, transparent and must tell us what is likely to happen in the future.

The next chapter deals with this in detail, but here are some ways that other organisations also measure customer service.

1. Repeat custom. Obviously, if this is rising, then your organisation is probably delivering great service and will continue to prosper in the future.

2. Average order size: Again, if this is rising, then you're probably doing things well. But, don't use this on its own. There may be many other reasons for this. This is a great measure, but only if it genuinely is as a result of customer delight.

3. Referrals: Measuring where new customers have come from is not only a good measure for customer service, but also is very helpful for measuring the effectiveness of any marketing. Whatever your organisation, this is a great measure, and should be undertaken no matter what. The only drawback is that it doesn't tell you WHY they've come to you, or what you're not doing well. We'll save this GREAT measure for the next chapter.

4. Complaints: Again, very important to measure, but hard to draw conclusions from.

   a. If complaints are falling, then is it because you're delivering better service, or is it because people are so fed up that they've stopped bothering to tell you, and instead are spending their time looking for an alternative?

   b. If they're rising, is it because you're getting worse, or are more people telling you things because they trust you more now?

   c. And remember: only about 1 in 10 people generally bother to complain, the others just go elsewhere and tell all their friends about you. Treat complaints as a compliment

11. **Awards**:

These are almost always worth bothering with. They have the following benefits:

   a. They motivate your people
   b. They build trust with your customer (but only if they have perceived value in your customer's eyes)
   c. They give you feedback on ways to improve
   d. They help you mix with industry leaders in your field
   e. They prove that you're 'above average' - which comes in particularly handy if you have a leased business and rents are linked to 'reasonable' maintainable trade

Yes, there's often a lot of paperwork involved with putting yourself forward for an award, yes it's a fiddle and yes, you're busy enough already, but do you want any of the above benefits?

And remember: most people don't bother to enter, so your chances are often very good.

12.   Other things:

a.   Tips: an obvious sign of customer service excellence

b.   Flowers: I know one organisation that specifically aims to deliver such great service that they regularly get bunches of flowers delivered. It happens so often, that they now measure this for a bit of fun!

Now wouldn't it be marvellous if we had a simple effective measure that would accurately predict success in all these areas, and give us valuable feedback to help us continually improve and motivate our people?

Read on!

Chapter Two: Measure Consistently and Obsessively

In writing this chapter, I have to start by acknowledging the great research contained within the book 'The Ultimate Question', by Bob Reichheld.

Before we get into this, please take two minutes to ask yourself why <u>you</u> personally usually don't fill in 'customer satisfaction surveys' for organisations when they ask you to? Write some thoughts down here:

<u>**Reasons why I personally rarely fill in 'customer satisfaction surveys':**</u>

How do I know you don't?

Simple: most people don't! So these surveys are usually a pointless exercise and heaven forbid anyone takes any action on any results from them!

[Note: this does not include focused surveys carried out on specific issues: these can be effective and produce useful information. I am talking here about 'general' 'customer satisfaction' surveys].

The customer is king. Those who please the customer best will win. When being surveyed, customers just want to tell you their views quickly and simply, not answer your questions. Winners are fanatical about enabling them to do this as easily as possible.

Here are the eleven key reasons why traditional customer satisfaction surveys don't work.

1. Too Long. The customer just wants to be listened to. They don't want to have to fill in loads of data.

2. Questions not Customer Focused. They're written by the Company. Come on - the customer just wants to feed back to you as easily as possible. they don't want to answer your questions!

3. It's marketing in disguise. The customer sees you want their phone number, email and inside leg measurement - they aren't fooled. They have enough 'spam' to deal with already and anyway, they don't want to tell you their age and what car they drive, they just want to tell you about your service.

4. It actually detracts from the customer service. Because the customer just wants to be 'listened' to and they don't do this!

5. Low response rates. Because of the above, response rates are usually very low (this is a huge issue). So the only people who end up telling you what they think are either those with a grudge, or those with time on their hands. Hardly likely to produce valuable information.

6. It produces no clear 'action points'. Because there are too many questions and not enough answers, often the data can be challenged, even if it did make sense. If it's good data, there's usually too little to break down meaningfully across Divisions or Departments.

7. It's out of date before it's published. These surveys are often an 'event', then the results are analysed (because they're too complicated), so by the time the average Joe sees them, they're a couple of months out of date and no use at all.

8. It actually makes the situation worse. Because of the above, what actually happens is that the wrong customers influence the decisions, the good customers don't bother and the employees just get fed up.

9. It doesn't identify the real issues. It's a lottery!

10. It produces no clear 'score'. So it has no real value.

11. Last, but not least, we don't want 'satisfied' customers; we want 'delighted' ones.

(There's a copy of this in Appendix 6).

So we don't want one of these do we? We want a 'greatness' survey. A simple, customer obsessed survey, that measures how 'great' the customer thinks we are and enables them to tell us what we can:

- Stop doing because it's 'poor'
- Keep doing because it's 'great'
- Start doing to become 'greater'

The key to measuring this is threefold:

1. Keep it simple (producing high response rates and helpful feedback)
2. Keep it present (ensuring the information is up to date and relevant)
3. Keep it obsessive (ensuring it produces real change for the better)

The system I propose should produce very high response rates with valuable feedback, and real incentives to help your people improve. It is a fantastic predictor of future success and has been proven many times. Best of all, it provides you with a clear 'customer delight score', very clear actions that are needed in order to increase this score and improve your business and best of all, this is not expensive to do.

But it is expensive not to do

This is it; a survey that is:

- Short: Three questions ONLY, informal and fun, anonymous where possible, with an extra section on the end to help the customer get resolution to any issues, and become a partner if they want to. You can even call it a '30 second questionnaire'. The customer will never object to this.

- Informal and fun: because this is not an inquest. This is a genuine desire to understand the customer so you can build trust and make his or her life easier. There's enough formal and boring paperwork around (just ask your local council to send you a sample), make this fun and interesting.

- Anonymous where possible: because you need to do everything in your power to maximise return rates and honesty of information, without which the whole process is basically a waste of everyone's time and anonymity boosts this significantly. Don't let your marketing department hijack this – this is customer feedback, not customer data collecting!

- Extra information: if you're gathering feedback with integrity, there's a good likelihood that the customer may want to share some thoughts with you on the feedback they gave, or even join a mailing list. If you're doing this with integrity, you can give them the opportunity to do this.

Question 1: The CFM Question

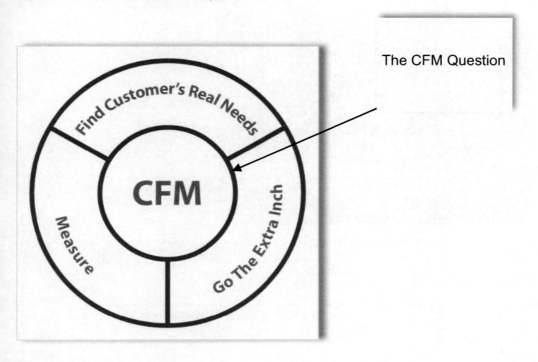

The CFM Question

In effect, this tells the customer what the CFM is (remember the CFM is written from the customer's point of view, so this should make sense to them, and if it doesn't, it's probably a good idea to have another look at it), and asks them how well they think you've done against it.

So what on earth is 'The CFM question'? To help you out here are some examples:

CFM	Possible CFM Questions
For every customer to leave with a smile, keen to return.	We want you to be leaving with a smile, keen to return, have we achieved this today?
To achieve 95% customer delight .	Our aim is to delight you, have we done that today?
98% on time in full.	We aim to give a completely reliable and high quality service; did we achieve this in your view?
The catch all (when you can't work out how to ask about the CFM).	Would you recommend us to a friend?

Alternatively, you can keep this fun and light hearted, which often improves response rates and adds to the customer experience.

Here's an example I've used:

"Our aim is for you to look like this when you leave. Did we achieve this today?"

The customer is asked to mark you on 1 out of 5 responses as follows:

This is then 'translated' as a score as follows.

Definitely not	Probably not	Maybe	Probably	Definitely

- 'Definitely not': you're 'poor'.
- 'Probably not' : you're 'poor'.
- 'Maybe': you're 'poor' but I'm too polite to tell you.
- 'Probably': you're 'satisfactory' - I don't think you're poor, but I don't think you're great. I'll remain a customer of yours only until someone better comes along.
- 'Definitely': you're 'great'. I want to do more business with you and tell my friends how 'great' you are.

Definitely not		Probably not		Maybe		Probably		Definitely	
1	2	3	4	5	6	7	8	9	10
POOR						'Satisfactory'		'Great'	

Alternatively, if you think it would be easier for your customer (depending on how your CFM is worded), you can ask them to mark you from 1 to 10, as shown above.

This now will give you a 'greatness' score!

Very simply:

- Take the total % of 'great' scores
- Take away the total % of 'poor' scores
- Gives you a % 'greatness' score

We call this a 'great or poor score'.

Note: you must ignore all who score you as 'satisfactory', as these neither benefit nor hinder your organisation. They are neutral.

The maximum score you can have is +100%, and the minimum is -100%.

When you measure this ongoing across the months (or weeks), you will then have very effective Key Performance Indicators to motivate and empower your people.

Here's an example of how this may look.

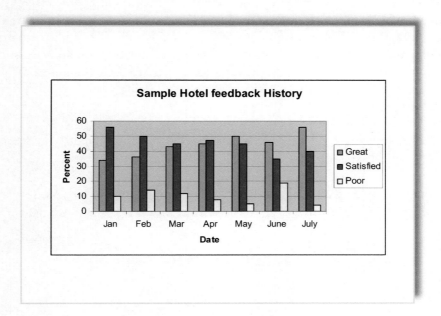

As you gather more and more data on this you can split this by department, depot, service, or individual (or whatever split is helpful to you), thus enabling you to catch people doing something well, spread best practice, and deal with poor performers before they affect bottom line figures.

So it's quite helpful.

Some organisations go as far as:

- Putting the score on people's badges at meetings.
- Having a policy that only those with a consistently above average score can be promoted.
- Having a large and lively scoreboard in the organisation's reception area.

Doing these sorts of things makes your message very clear and ensures you consistently deliver and develop ever higher levels of customer service excellence.

It also adds value to the customer, because it enhances your relationship with them (even if you've not done a very good job in the first place) and proves to them that you do actually care and are trying to listen to them and improve around their needs.

In fact, I would argue that, in order to make this live and work properly within your organisation (and not just be lip service), you should do these things:

1. Tell everyone what you're trying to do.
2. Clarify your CFM (obviously).
3. Start measuring. (This will be a 'kick start' that will do three things:
   a. Show your people that you're serious,
   b. Show your customers that you're serious,
   c. Help you clarify what the customer REALLY wants).
4. Readdress the CFM and your people's involvement after the first round of measuring.
5. Keep measuring.
6. Have the weekly 'accountability' meetings (as detailed in the previous chapter).
7. Start the process of refining ALL your strategy, policy, procedure and behaviour around the CFM. This would include taking the CFM measurement score as a key indicator of performance, pay and promotion.
8. Keep measuring and keep refining (this is like a 'flywheel' driving your business, the more you focus on and keep turning it, the more it will add power and velocity to your organisation.

It's so simple. That's why it's so powerful.

A good example of continual refinement of service, based on customer feedback is contained in a recent email I received from Amazon.com. It stated:

> "FREE supersaver delivery and Amazon Prime are examples of our obsession with new innovations on behalf of our customers. We strive every day to lower prices and speed up delivery."

Question 2

What, logically, would you like to ask your customers next? Of course.

"Why did you give us this score?"

You can use whatever words suit you and your situation best, but basically you want to know what it was about your service that made them give you this score.   They will give you a HUGE amount of helpful qualitative information in this sector. Much will be brief and just confirm what you know, but in this there will be some real nuggets to help you drive your service forward.

It again adds value to the customer, because it further enhances your relationship and proves to them that you do actually care and are trying to listen to them and improve around their needs.   This will also give you the ammunition you need to 'catch your people doing something well' (as mentioned before).

This qualitative feedback can then be split into three action points alongside the grouping of the score.

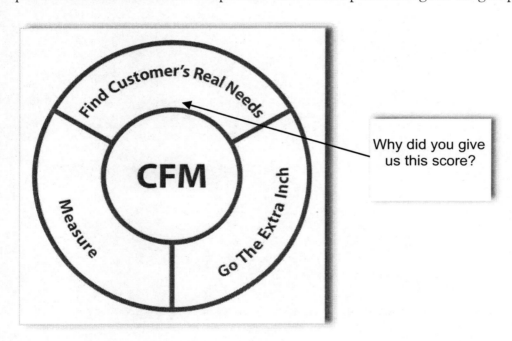

So this system provides you with fantastically helpful information to run your organisation better through enhanced customer service.

Group	What do you do with the feedback
Great	Make sure you spread this as great practice, and put systems in place to ensure it always happens.
Satisfied	Tells you what you could do to build your organisation, through improved service, in the future (but don't have to do urgently).
Poor	Tells you two things: • things you must sort out very quickly to prevent damage to your organisation; • who the customers are that you're never going to please (so you can manage their expectations better, and those of others like them).

Question 3

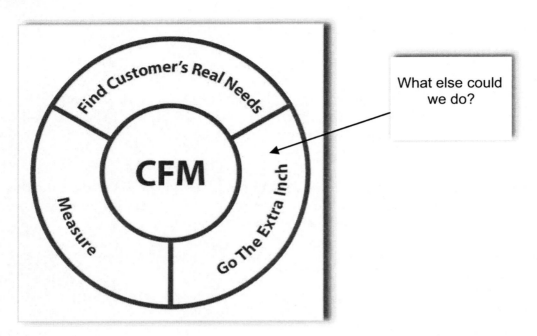

This is the question that elicits just a bit more information from the customer about how else you could improve in the future. It will go a bit like this:

"Is there anything else we could do to make

- **your life easier**
- **your experience better**

next time?"

Notice the wording of the question is based on how can we 'go the extra inch?'

The joy of this question comes when you have the majority of responses in 'great' or 'satisfied' (as you should have), in that, they will probably tell you about the good stuff you do in the response to Question 2.

But you'd also like to know how you could best improve the service you give; otherwise you could get the false impression that all is hunky dory and you just need to sit on your laurels. Even those who think you're 'poor' will often give helpful information in this question.

On top of this, it again adds value to the relationship with the customer, as it says 'we're serious about improvement and we want to listen to your ideas'. **Customers love this.**

So you collate the answers to this question, by group, to see what you can do to improve your service further. You'll find this question really provides some meat for you to get your teeth into.

Other Questions

<u>Don't ask them.</u>

Go for quantity of replies to get to the real issues, not quantity of questions.

You can do two other things however:

Firstly: if you're using a third party to do this survey (which is far more effective, see below) they can ask your customer if they'd like you to contact them about the feedback. If you do this, and you have the capability and the desire (at all levels) to actually make the calls and listen to the feedback, you can use this to repair irrepairable issues, and build fantastically good customer relationship (in the same way as you would do in dealing with complaints).

Remember: issues handled well have the ability to create a fantastic customer experience and build significant loyalty.

Here's a sample phrase you might use on a written feedback request:

> *"This information will ONLY be used to measure and improve the service we give. If you'd like us to contact you about your feedback, please let us have your contact name and number here."*

Secondly: you can ask them if they'd like their email address to be added to your newsletter marketing lists. This gives them the option to opt in if they want to (and many do), but does not impose or ask for the email address for any other reason. The great thing is, that if they choose to give you their email address, they'll probably look at and respond to offers you send them, so it makes your marketing in this area much more targeted, and less of a 'shotgun' approach.

Here's some sample phrases you might use:

> *'Please add your email address here if you'd like to be added to our mailing list'.*

> *'If you'd like us to keep in contact with offers and news, please do let us have your email address here.'*

> *'Become a XXXXX VIP! Write your email address here and we'll make sure you're the first to know of any special offers.'*

Always remember, the purpose of these two extra pieces of information is SOLELY to add value to your service, NOT to gather contact information. Customers generally don't want you to have these details and if you ask for them as a matter of course, without integrity to the above principles, you'll kill the whole system.

Methods of Delivery

The joy of this simple system also lies in its ease of delivery. It can be done:

- In person
- By phone
- On the web
- By post

In person: this has the advantage of being direct and gives you the ability to find out some really valuable information, but it has the disadvantage of being a bit off-putting to the customer if not handled excellently and very expensive in time and resources.

I would generally only recommend this for specific research or to really understand the customer's needs and desires for a new project, or to finalise your CFM and ensure its accuracy.

By phone: this has the advantage of being direct and gives you the ability to probe and find out some useful information, but it has the disadvantage of sometimes catching the customer at an inconvenient moment, when they may not be wanting to give you feedback. However, because the system is so simple, short, and completely customer focused, I personally have never yet had anyone refuse to answer the three questions. Once you get hold of the people you need to speak to, this method will generally have a greater than 90% success rate if handled professionally and sensitively.

On the web: this has the advantage of being easy to set up and convenient to the customer, but has the disadvantage of having very low (and biased) response rates and is wide open to abuse, so is not really reliable (as you see on websites that 'gather' customer feedback, the level is often very low and therefore usually not reliable or helpful). Customers generally won't want to log on to give you their feedback, they'll just go somewhere else with their custom. The best exceptions to this are sites like Ebay, where the whole system works (brilliantly) by way of feedback.

By post: this is by far the best method from the customer's point of view, as they can tell you what they think as and when it suits them. However, it will have lower response rates than the first two methods. When handled badly, response rates can be as low as 5% (not quite as bad as 'customer satisfaction surveys' which are often 2% or below), but handled positively and enthusiastically by well trained staff and as part of an ongoing system supported by all personnel, this can easily enjoy response rates of 30% +. This system also has the advantage of being very cost effective and simple to organise.

However all of these work much better if they're done by a professional and focused, third party.

Here are some reasons why it's usually better to get a third party to do this for you.

1. **Honesty of data.** The customer just wants to tell you what they think, honestly, without embarrassment or upset. The ONLY way you can be sure of this is via an anonymous survey conducted by a third party.

2. **Provides perspective.** The third party will see the feedback just as it is and will be able to see the issues clearly and from an unbiased but expert perspective. No matter how objective you think you are, you'll filter feedback through your own emotions and desires.

3. **Cost-effective use of time and resources**. Your expertise lies in providing your service. Using a third party to collate and provide customer feedback is both cost-effective in time, and avoids distraction and bias. Your energies are best used dealing with the feedback to improve your business, not in gathering it.

4. **Ensures integrity to the customer's needs and desires**. Again, no matter how 'objective' you are, you won't be able to resist the odd extra question here and there. This will destroy the exercise in the customer's view. The customer just wants you to listen to them - nothing else!

5. **High response rates**. If you're paying for the service, you'll want to use it as much as possible. If you do it yourself it'll just be a chore and your mindset will be the opposite.

6. **A regular report with a 'score'.** Only a third party can give you an objective score for you to use to motivate and encourage your people. Only a third party will always produce a full report. If you do it, you may be tempted to cut corners in these vital areas.

7. **Peace of mind.** Using a third party ensures it gets done on time every time and takes away another worry from you.

8. **Resource.** Using a customer service specialist means that you'll benefit from their input and resources to improve your business.

9. **Shows you're serious.** Using a third party shows that you really do want to know what your customer thinks and that you're prepared to invest money and time with a professional to do this. This builds loyalty in itself.

Remember: **We don't want 'satisfied' customers, we want 'delighted' ones.**

Sometimes the best way to handle this is a two pronged approach.

- First prong: after each transaction, check with the customer, by asking questions such as:

    1. How was everything?
    2. Is there anything else we can do?

This is a simple and effective system to promote and enhance service, and to avoid problems turning into disasters. It always amazes me that a simple system such as this is so rarely built into organisations' operational procedures. Restaurants seem to do this as a matter of course and garages seem to have started doing it, but most other organisations don't seem to have even considered it. Sometimes they say it's too, difficult, time consuming, or expensive to do this, yet these same organisations spend fortunes on sales and marketing trying to gain new customers.

- Second prong: use a third party to 'audit' this, using the 'great or poor' method outlined above. Producing a score, going deeper into analysis and issues, and providing unbiased and expert feedback on the findings.

This way you get the best of both worlds.

Does this measure work? Yes, just try it.

You can even start the whole process of customer service excellence development from here. Just start measuring, have weekly meetings to discuss the results, then the different behaviour and improved service will start to materialise. With your CFM and principles as your compass and this book as your map you'll be unstoppable.

Just try it.

To Conclude

- Great customer service is the single most effective way to build turnover and profits
- What gets measured gets done
- Most customer surveys don't measure what matters and have little positive motivational effect
- Using this system is an effective answer to this key need
- This system allows you to:
- Focus service accountability
  - Take action on good and bad results
  - Motivate and empower staff to deliver results
  - Promote empowerment & responsibility
  - Identify profitable customers
  - Measure and incentivise progress in 'real time'
- And thereby build turnover and profits
  - (Even public and not-for-profit organisations can use this effectively, as it simply predicts future success and effectiveness around the CFM)

And also consider:

From the customer's point of view, they know that you won't get it right 100% of the time, but, in their eyes

The real crime is not the 'getting it wrong', but
The 'not listening and caring'

This will resolve that.

For example: if you're a hotel, give bad service and don't handle it well, the recipient of the bad service may well put a negative comment about you on 'tripadvisor.com' for all the world to see. However, if you run the above mentioned system, you'll have given them their opportunity to have their say and you'll be in a great position to resolve the issue, thus avoiding their need to resort to public humiliation.

Websites giving the public the ability to humiliate you to the entire world will just get more and more commonplace. You need to adopt this solution before it happens to you.

Just try it.

To round off this chapter, I leave you with two things:

1.   The other fantastic benefit of proper and obsessive measuring is that it keeps you focused on your Customer Focused Mission.   So everyone knows every day in every action what is required of them, and there is no confusion.

It also means that you keep checking that your CFM is correct and relevant. These things may change and develop over time, so it's essential to keep measuring the checking.

In a nutshell, it turns the 4 key action points into a sort of 'flywheel' to give momentum and speed to your organisation, and keep it constantly developing and improving in the right direction, with your CFM as the hub.

It looks like this:

Conversely, if you don't measure this, it is very likely that it will be seen as a 'flavour of the month' and will probably get lost when you hit your next crisis. We don't want this.

Just try it!   (And remember, to display the score prominently and obsessively).

2.   Some Quotes:

A Native American elder once described his own inner struggles in this manner: *"Inside of me there are two dogs. One of the dogs is mean and evil. The other dog is good. The mean dog fights the good dog all the time."* When asked which dog wins, he reflected for a moment and replied, *"the one I feed the most."*

"The only man who behaved sensibly was my tailor; he took my measurement anew every time he saw me, while all the rest went on with their old measurements and expected them to fit me." - George Bernard Shaw

"I have six honest serving men, they taught me all I knew. Their names are 'what' and 'why' and 'when' and 'how' and 'where' and 'who'." - Rudyard Kipling

"There are two possible outcomes: if the result confirms the hypothesis, then you've made a measurement. If the result is contrary to the hypothesis, then you've made a discovery." - Enrico Fermi.

Chapter Three: Précis

The basics of the book in 6 pages to help you remember and pass on the key learning points without having to re-read the whole book each time.

Issue 1:   **How happy do customers have to be in order for your customer service to build your turnover, increase margins and reduce costs?**

Issue 2:   **How much is all this worth in the real world?**

Issue 3:   **Customer service always seems like 'blindingly obvious common sense'. The real issue, which is rarely addressed is 'why is it so often not common practice?'**

Issue 4:   **How can we address this?**

Issue 5:   **What tools do we need?**

Issue 6:   **How do we make this live on a daily basis?**

The answer to all these, after many months of research, is profoundly simple, yet profoundly hard to make work. It's easy to understand, but have you got the guts and willpower to make it work? It's up to you.

The Issue	The Answer
How happy do customers have to be in order for your customer service to build your turnover, increase margins and reduce costs?	In a nutshell: delighted. In effect, if you're not 'great' then you'll be 'poor', in your customer's eyes.
How much is all this worth in the real world?	A fortune. Studies show that investment in customer service excellence is at least six times as effective as investment in sales and marketing.
Customer service always seems like 'blindingly obvious common sense'. The real issue, which is rarely addressed is 'why is it so often not common practice?'	Organisations are not built and organised ruthlessly around a 'Customer Focused Mission', so the customer is only seen as an important person in the organisation when the finance director isn't shouting!
How can we address this?	There are two main things to do: 1. Develop a 'Customer Focused Mission'. 2. Make sure you understand the REAL needs of your customer, then align all strategy, processes and systems around your Mission.
What tools do we need?	Some simple but effective tools to help you 'go the extra inch'.
How do we make this live on a daily basis?	By measuring, reporting, developing and holding people accountable (for good and bad), around the Customer Focused Mission.

A few more details on all of these:

In effect, if you're not 'great' then you'll be 'poor', in your customer's eyes.

- As a customer, we expect the plane to get us to our destination in one piece and basically on time: this will 'satisfy' us. But how often have you heard someone sing the praises of, and recommend an airline just because of this? Never.

- You know that, as a customer, you have to be 'wowed' in order to recommend a product or service to someone else. A 'satisfied' customer is not good enough.

- Good service results in average results. The only way to develop great results (short of spending a fortune on marketing and selling), is to 'wow' the customer consistently. In effect, you're either 'great' or you're 'poor'.

- If you don't 'wow' the customer, your only alternative is to spend a fortune on sales and marketing. This will keep you 'poor'. The only way to deliver 'wow' service consistently and excellently is to have a watertight system that doesn't stifle individuals' creativity and flair.

- Doing this well will result in great results for a small financial cost and we all want that. This book (and the training we offer alongside it), delivers this.

Investment in customer service excellence pays back at least 6 times the rate of investment in sales and marketing.

Here are the facts:

1. It costs an average of **6 times** as much to attract a new customer as to keep an existing one.
2. On average, dissatisfied customers tell **10-16 people** about their negative experiences.
3. Of customers who switch to a competitor, up to **80%** say that they were 'satisfied' before making the switch!
4. **91%** of unhappy customers won't buy again from a company that displeased them.

Organisations are not built and organised ruthlessly around a 'Customer Focused Mission' (CFM).

So what happens when the needs of the customer conflicts with the needs of:

- The shareholders
- The boss
- The system
- The last few weeks of the financial year
- The employee who wants to get home on time

Without a 'Customer Focused Mission' to which ALL THINGS, from the shareholders and MD's needs downwards, are subjugated, the customer's needs will not often be heard or met, and your service will be patchy at best. I know this is a hard pill to swallow, but you know it's true.

It's much easier to see it and comment on it in other organisations when you're the customer … it's quite another thing entirely to reorganise your organisation / department / unit / self around a CFM.

Developing and ruthlessly sticking to a 'Customer Focused Mission'

In order to develop a CFM you need to ensure all stakeholders, without exception, are aligned around the 'Customer Focused Vision'.

And the 'Customer Focused Vision' should be something like:

'The only way we'll succeed is if we delight the customer consistently and excellently. The only way we'll do this is by having the guts and passion to do what's best for the customer at all times, even if it may conflict with short term goals.'

Focus on the customers and the results will follow - not the other way round.

Understanding the REAL needs of your customer, and aligning all strategy, processes and systems around the CFM.

We think we know what the customer wants, but we don't. Customers make logical decisions based on emotional stimuli. In a word, they're 'unpredictable'. So it's very hard to anticipate their needs, yes, but we CAN predict their EMOTIONS.

For example: if I go out to eat in a restaurant, I don't want a meal (I can get that far easier and cheaper in a shop), I want:

Relaxation / to be looked after / some time out / a quiet meeting / romance / etc.

So the restaurant, in order to deliver excellent service to me (and therefore fulfil its CFM), needs to work out what emotions I'll have if the above things happen?

Probably 'happy and relaxed'!

So they need to align ALL strategy, processes, and systems around making the experience 'happy and relaxed' for the customer. Yes, the quality of the food, service and environment are important in themselves, but ONLY in as far as they produce 'happy and relaxed' feelings in the customer.

So often organisations spend a huge amount of time, effort and money in things that have no bearing on the customer's emotions, and precious little on the things that do (perhaps like answering the phone quickly and efficiently). This is because they haven't thought this through, and haven't got a system to keep listening to the customers (at the deeper level).

So, all you need to do, in order to delight your customers excellently and consistently, is to think through what EMOTIONS your customer will display if you get it very right (i.e. deliver your CFM), then align all strategy, processes and behaviour around generating this, then keep listening.

'Going the Extra Inch'

Customer service material so often mentions going the 'extra mile', but this makes it seem hard and onerous, and it shouldn't be: it should be easy and fun. The customer will be wowed by the little extras delivered excellently, consistently and positively, rather than the great things (that are so much harder to get excellent and consistent).

You can take a horse to water, but you can't make it drink. So it is with your people. You can tell them to 'go the extra inch', but you can't make them. In fact, the more you tell them, the less likely it is that they'll want to do it!

The only way you can get them to 'go the extra inch', excellently consistently and positively, is by:

- Developing your CFM
- Aligning everything around it
- Empowering and encouraging
- Measuring and feeding back
- And of course, leading by example

Measuring the CFM

What gets measured gets done.

It's exactly the same with customer service, but most customer service measurements are lame and pointless at best, and very often have the opposite effect to that intended.

This is because:

- They ask the wrong questions
- They have low response rates
- They have no meaningful score
- They are not regular enough
- They provide little helpful feedback
- They look for 'satisfaction' (and we don't want this!)

The key is to ask the customer:

1. Have we achieved our CFM?
2. Why?
3. What else could we do to improve your experience?

If we ask these questions, we'll have the score, along with the qualitative feedback we need to develop our organisation towards excellence.

And remember, doing this type of surveying is an area where the input of a third party can really help you. It will give you high quality honest information, a meaningful score, perspective on your business, high response rates, regularity, and, above all peace of mind. Using a third party is also a huge message to all within the organisation that you're serious about getting this right - and it can be done very cost-effectively.

Reporting, developing and holding people accountable (for good and bad), around the Customer Focused Mission.

Once you've done all the above, you need to be persistent and consistent in order to show that you're serious. Otherwise it has the amazingly high probability as being seen as a 'flavour of the month', and something to do for a while and then get back to 'business as usual'.

In order to avoid this, you need to:

- Consistently adapt and develop strategy, processes and systems around the CFM: this is a journey not a destination.
- Measure as shown above: preferably monthly at the minimum.
- Make the measurement one of the key success indicators in your organisation.
- Publish the measurement in a clear and prominent way.
- Meet regularly within your department / group / team (I'd suggest weekly for 15 – 20 minutes only), specifically to discuss this issue: How are we doing? What's going well? What needs improving? What can we do this week to 'go an extra inch'?
- Hold EVERYONE accountable, for good and bad, all the time.

Here's a view of the future:

We are in the middle of a Social Revolution, even greater in impact than the Industrial Revolution. The Internet, and explosion of information it has generated, will empower the customer unlike anything that has gone before. It has also created a truly global economy.

On top of this, the customer previously disempowered and abused by misleading adverts and clever marketing, will become ever more demanding and unforgiving.

'Satisfied' customers are no longer good enough. Cutting edge service is winning business globally at an astonishing pace and 'traditional' businesses are becoming extinct almost overnight. In order to prosper in the future, an organisation's service must be 'great', because, if not, it'll be 'poor'.

For companies to thrive (or even survive) in this brave new world, they MUST be very clear on what they are trying to deliver to the customer, and listen and react to their customers' views and needs.

Existing systems and mindsets make this very hard for organisations to deal with. 'Great or Poor' fills this gap and gives them the mindset, skills and tools to thrive in the future.

So here's the plan in four easy steps:

1. Develop a 'Customer Focused Mission'.
2. Understand the REAL needs of your customer and then align all strategy, processes and behaviour around your CFM.
3. 'Go the extra inch'.
4. Measure progress, report back, and hold people accountable.

Do this very well and consistently and your results will increase significantly.

Chapter Four: Action

Knowledge without action means: **NOTHING**

In the same way that there's no point in being able to read if you don't read.

So please use this chapter to write in your action plans and then share these with someone else. Ask the other person to review this with you on a regular basis (start monthly, then move to quarterly).

Research shows that **95% of you won't do this**. You'll put this book away and carry on as before.

Be the top 5% who do.

The world is changing too fast. You need to remember Darwin's law.

**It is not the strongest of the species, nor the most intelligent,
that survives,
but the one most responsive to change**

Be in the 5% of survivors, not in the 95% of strugglers.

Make the commitment today. Phone someone who you can share ideas and concerns with (this is often a third party in a work environment).

Phone that person NOW!

Item	Plan	Date to Address
Getting a coach.	Phone a third party and share these ideas and commit to action.	NOW

Actions agreed	Timescale and Comments

Item	Plan	Date to Address
Why are we in business?	Find out why your organisation does what it does: what is the service that needs to be fulfilled from the customer's point of view. Try asking customers their views. And how about your colleagues?	1 Week

Actions agreed	Timescale and Comments

Item	Plan	Date to Address
Does everyone know how their role fits with the above?	Once you've clarified the above, start asking around, and keep at it until universal clarity is reached.	

Actions agreed		Timescale and Comments

Item	Plan	Date to Address
Mission Questions.	Refer back to the questions about the CFM. What does this tell you? What actions do you now need to take? Are you a thirsty enough horse to be 'great' in your role? And, if not, what are you going to do about it?	

Actions agreed		Timescale and Comments

Item	Plan	Date to Address
Have we got the right people for the job?	What can I do to change the people? Whose help will I need? What actions do I need to take now? And ongoing?	

Actions agreed	Timescale and Comments

Item	Plan	Date to Address
What are my habits?	Do the exercise on habits (Pages 18-19).	

Actions agreed	Timescale and Comments

Item	Plan	Date to Address
The cost and opportunity of great customer service.	Take a lot of time to consider and work out how much poor customer service REALLY costs your organisation. Then do some figures to work out the impact of a few key issues being addressed, and thereby significantly improving your customer service. Share this with a senior person. Agree a pilot at the very least! Use the DR GRAC form to work out these actions. (See Appendix)	

Actions agreed	Timescale and Comments
Pilot agreed:	Date:

Item	Plan	Date to Address
The lifetime value of my customer.	Do the exercise on lifetime value of my customer. Get team to do the same exercise. Meet and share results. Share with your boss.	

Actions agreed	Timescale and Comments

Item	Plan	Date to Address
Process	Examine all your processes from the point of view of the CFM. Do they add to or subtract from the CFM? Do we know how the customer experiences them? What changes might we consider? In an ideal world, what processes would deliver the CFM fantastically? What small steps can we make now to proceed towards this CFM focused picture?	ONGOING

Actions agreed	Timescale and Comments

Item	Plan	Date to Address
Decisions.	Commit today to filtering ALL your decisions through the CFM. Tell all your associates and colleagues.	NOW

Actions agreed	Timescale and Comments
Where are the potential conflicts with strategy and processes?	

Item	Plan	Date to Address
Time Effectiveness	Measure your time effectiveness against the ideas shown in the Appendix. If you need some help in this area: book it today!	NOW

Actions agreed	Timescale and Comments

Item	Plan	Date to Address
Effective Communication.	Re-read the section on communication, as this is the area where customer service most often falls down. Commit today to: • Return ALL calls within 24 hours • Deal with email effectively • Personalise your answer machine / voicemail every day	NOW

Actions agreed	Timescale and Comments

Item	Plan	Date to Address
Listening Skills.\	Commit to practice this every day. Effective listening is one of the most powerful skills you can possess.	NOW

Record of effective listening achieved	Outcome

Item	Plan	Date to Address
Acres of Diamonds Story.	Relate this at your next team meeting and then explain why you're telling it.	

Actions agreed	Timescale and Comments

Item	Plan	Date to Address
Catch people doing something well.	Commit to catch someone at home and someone at work EVERY DAY. This is also a hugely powerful skill at home.	NOW

Record of 'catching' achieved	Outcome

Item	Plan	Date to Address
Ongoing Study.	Plan to continue study of how to improve your work and life effectiveness. Commit to one book from the list in the Appendix every month for a year. At the end of 12 months you will have transformed your life.	ONGONG

Books to Read	Timescale and Comments
1	
2	
3	
4	
5	
6	
7	
8	
9	
10	
11	
12	

Item	Plan	Date to Address
Start Measuring.	Even if you can't do this for your whole organisation, work within your circle of influence and start measuring the part that you can. It's not time consuming and it's not expensive. Before you start, tell everyone what you're doing and why, and invite them to either be part of the pilot or help you analyse and learn from the results.	

Actions Agreed:	Timescale and Comments

If you need help with this, please go to www.customer-service.championsclubcommunity.com/

Item	Plan	Date to Address
Clear and obsessive scoreboard.	Set up a clear and obsessive scoreboard. Update it regularly.	

Actions agreed	Timescale and Comments

Item	Plan	Date to Address
Weekly accountability meetings.	Start weekly meetings with my team.	

Actions agreed		Timescale and Comments

Item	Plan	Date to Address
Start Again.	Read this book again and restart the actions.	In 6 month's time.

Now, phone back your coach, tell them the outline of your plans and set the date for the first meeting.

Remember: *"An ounce of action is worth a ton of theory."* - *Ralph Waldo Emerson*

You're on the way.

Good Luck!

And if you need help we're there for you at http://customer-service.championsclubcommunity.com

Do not follow the herd, for where the herd has gone the grass is all eaten. - Bob Dylan

APPENDICES

APPENDIX ONE: Vision, Mission and Values and the difference between them

I have come across much confusion (not least in my own mind) about the difference between 'Vision' and 'Mission' and 'Values'. So here's a quick and easy clarification.

VISION

A 'VISION', is an 'idea', often called a 'dream' or an 'inspiration', that keeps entrepreneurs awake at night, inspires the foundation of organisations and drives them to achieve their 'dream'.   It's the 'why we do what we do'.

It is the thinking and inspiration behind the 'MISSION': i.e. It explains why the 'MISSION' is the 'MISSION', and, without this thinking, the 'MISSION' is all too often empty, meaningless (and often focused on only one stakeholder's needs - no prizes for guessing whose).

For it to be a truly empowering and successful 'VISION' it needs four intertwining elements:

1. Passion
2. Clarity
3. Worthwhile purpose and
4. Customer Focused.

1. **Passion**: the owner needs to be passionate about it. Without this, it will never reach it's full potential.

2. **Clarity**: it needs to paint a very clear picture of the future. The ability to do this is vital and is the root of success in all great visions: the power of a 'clear picture' can be seen in the following situations:

    Muhammad Ali: visualised the whole fight, and even the round and minute when he would knock his opponent out, BEFORE the fight.

    Martin Luther King: 'I have a dream … that the sons of former slaves and former slave owners, will be able to sit down together at the table of brotherhood'.

    Note: these are both very clear PICTURES of the future - not just WORDS.

To see how important this is, then just try these two simple exercises:

i.   Think of the word 'apple': did you see a picture of the fruit in your mind or the word 'apple'? The picture, of course!

ii. Get a bank piece of paper and follow these simple instructions. Then I'll tell you what picture I was instructing you to draw.

-   Start at the bottom left hand corner
-   Draw a short horizontal line to the right
-   Then a vertical line upwards
-   Then ¾ of a circle
-   Then a vertical line downwards
-   Then a short horizontal line to the right
-   Then a vertical line upwards
-   Then a line 135 degrees to the right
-   Then a line at a right angle to that downwards
-   Then a vertical line downwards
-   And lastly another small horizontal line to the right
-   Finished!

What have you got?

Is it a basic outline of a house with a tree on the left hand side?

It isn't?

What on earth were you doing? I gave you clear instructions!

Can you see this scenario repeating itself every day at work? Of course you can - so now you know how VITAL a CLEAR PICTURE is when setting a VISION!

Here's the picture to put you out of your misery.

3. **'Significant' or 'worthwhile' purpose**: it needs to connect directly with people's 'need for significance' in the world. If it's about exploiting a loophole to make a quick buck, that may be successful in the short term, but won't stand the test of time. If the VISION has this 'worthwhile purpose' it will invigorate and embolden employees to excellence, and thus be a key building block of an organisation's success.

4. **Customer Focused**: we might make the greatest widgets in the world, but if they are of no value to the customer, there's not much point. The VISION has to be from the 'customer's' point of view, because otherwise it's a great but often a bit pointless idea (remember the Sinclair C5?). In order to do this, we have to know who our target audience is: the clearer we are on this, the simpler this (very difficult) step becomes.

Some examples of a 'translation' of point 4 into the customer's point of view:

	The 'traditional' view of the business	Who is the target customer?	The customer's point of view
Pub Restaurant	Providing food and drink	People who enjoy food within 20 miles radius	Providing an enjoyable experience
Insurance Company	Providing the best cover at the best price	Everyone in a certain group in a certain area	Providing peace of mind
News Broadcaster	Providing a wide coverage of news	Everyone in a certain group in a certain area	Providing entertainment
Public Body	Provider of public services	The people to whom they are answerable	Improving the quality of life
Space Agency	Getting to the moon	The citizens of the country and most of the world	Pride, passion and Technological advancement

A 'VISION' is something that ALL the stakeholders can clearly understand and mentally 'buy in to', thus binding them into a team that's 'pulling in the same direction'.

Problems occur:

- If the 'VISION' isn't clearly there: then the stakeholders make it up in their own mind (engendering confusion at best and dysfunctional cross purposes at worst).
- If the 'VISION' isn't based on 'worthwhile' causes: this starts a cancer that eats away at the organisation and eventually kills it.
- If management isn't passionate about it: it won't engender commitment.
- If management takes actions that are contrary to it: actions speak louder than words!
- If there isn't a 'clear picture' that all can 'see': otherwise it'll be open to interpretation, depending on the angle of the person looking at it. (e.g. 'To be the leading … (anything)', what does 'leading' actually mean?).

Examples of a successful 'VISION'

Amazon.com: *'Our Vision is to be earth's most customer centric company; to build a place where people can come to find and discover anything they might want to buy online.'*

- Passion
- Clarity
- Worthwhile purpose
- Stated from the customer's point of view

This is short, clear and concise (and very bold), and thus empowers the employees. In my view this is a 'VISION' and 'MISSION' built into one, because it's so simple and clear, there is no need for a separate 'MISSION' explaining how we're going to make the 'VISION' work.

Merck: *'Medicine is for the people, it is not for the profits. If we look after the people well enough, the profits will follow'*

- Passion
- Clarity
- Worthwhile purpose
- Stated from the customer's point of view

The Monkton Inn: *'Many pubs offer poor quality at cheap prices, or good quality at expensive prices. We believe pubs should offer the best quality and best service at the most competitive price possible. That way, they become a place where people return to again and again, and tell all their friends. This is what we are trying to achieve at the Monkton'.*

- Passion
- Clarity
- Worthwhile purpose
- Stated from the customer's point of view

Great or Poor - Excellence in Customer Service: *'Satisfied' customers are no longer good enough: cutting edge service is winning business globally at an astonishing pace, and 'traditional' businesses are becoming extinct almost overnight. In order to prosper in the future, an organisation's service must be 'great', because, if not, it'll be 'poor'.*

For companies to thrive (or even survive) in this brave new world, they MUST listen, and react to their customers' views and needs. Existing systems and mindsets make this very hard for organisations to deal with. Great or Poor fills this gap, and gives them the knowledge and tools to thrive in the future.

- Passion
- Clarity
- Worthwhile purpose
- Stated from the customer's point of view

This is much longer, but clearly shows the thinking behind the business, thus giving 'purpose' and 'meaning' to the 'MISSION'.

MISSION

This is much easier: a 'MISSION' is:

- what we're going to do in order to deliver the 'VISION'
- what result we want from our customers
- and is often accompanied by 'VALUES', which mean how we're going to do it

When an organisation has these clearly thought through and clearly communicates them incessantly, to all stakeholders, they will then have 'alignment' and the foundations of success will be in place.

But beware: this takes

- time
- effort
- involvement

And cannot be 'done overnight', and just communicated to the people:

No involvement = no commitment

You will know when this really is working when everyone from the MD to the loo cleaner (both roles being equally important), can clearly state the MISSION when asked, and can understand and find guidance in it for their role.

The story goes of the person sweeping out the hangar at NASA who, when asked what his role was, replied: *'I am helping to put a man on the moon'.*

Bingo!

A great Mission statement must be:

- Clear (easy to understand for all stakeholders)
- Empowering (empowers all stakeholders to make decisions based on the 'MISSION')
- Measurable (the measurement as shown in this book)
- Worthwhile (otherwise it will destroy the organisation)
- Directly linked to the VISION (obviously)
- Customer focused - say no more!

And very often, a great Mission statement should be:

- Timeless: it should be able to stand the test of time, and will usually achieve this by being based on timeless principles

Examples of a successful 'MISSION'

- **A council**: To improve the quality of life for all residents and visitors.
- **An accountancy business**: 'To deliver a service that exceeds customers' expectations'.
- **A Pub Restaurant**: 'For all customers to leave with a smile on their face, keen to return again'.
- **NASA**: 'To put a man on the moon before the end of the decade'
- **Tesco**: 'Every little helps!'

An example of an unsuccessful 'MISSION':

Ratners.

During the 1980s Gerald Ratner built his Ratner's business into the world's biggest brand of jewellery, through a series of publicity stunts and takeover deals. In 1991, however, Ratner managed to destroy his brand in the space of a sentence. In a speech to the Institute of Directors in London, he said the secret to Ratner's success was that many of its items of jewellery were 'total crap'.

He also joked that Ratners earrings were likely to last for less time than a Marks & Spencer sandwich. Although the room filled with laughter, Ratner's investors and customers couldn't see the joke. Shortly afterwards he backtracked, saying that he was referring only to a very few items, but the damage had been done.

The Ratner's brand name became synonymous with 'crap' products and a lack of respect for its customers. The Company's share price plummeted from £2 to less than 8p, and consumer confidence sank without trace. Group profits fell from £112 million in 1991 to losses of £122 million a year later.

And here's a great example of a 'VISION' that's been confused by its own organisation as a 'MISSION'.

Ikea.

The Swedish Company's Mission statement is "to create a better everyday life for the many people by developing good quality, functional and well-designed products at prices so low that the many people can afford them".

If asked (unlikely, I admit), I'd seek to convince them that this definitely is a 'VISION' (and a very good one), but the 'MISSION' should be something like:

'More than 95% of customers rave about their new furniture to their friends'.

VALUES

This is also easy, these are: **how we're going to do it.**

The word 'value' means: 'the quality of the thing that makes it important or desirable'.

Values are guidelines for the people in the organisation, usually based on deeply held beliefs. They need to be clearly described, so the organisation can identify exactly the actions needed to demonstrate the Values, in order to achieve these actions, they need to be measured.

Having clear Values also enables the organisation to attract like minded people to help it grow, indeed they should form the basis of all recruitment and appraisal processes.

But please note: **Unless the behaviour of ALL in the organisation reflects the Values at ALL times, the Values are less than meaningless**

In fact they then become a hindrance.

Examples of Values working well:

Johnson & Johnson

Value: *'Profit comes behind quality products'*

When they had a problem with the quality of a product, they withdrew it immediately, at significant expense.

Merck:

Value: *'medicine is for the people, it is not for the profits'*

When they developed a drug for river blindness that no one who was in an area affected by river blindness could afford, they developed it anyway, and then gave it away free.

Examples of Values working badly:

- A company I once worked for:

  Value: 'The customer is the most important person in the business'

  The customer services director regularly failed to phone customers (and colleagues) back, when they phoned him about issues or complaints.

- Organisations that put the directors' car parking spaces closest to the entrance.

- Directors who have a strict car policy for most of the organisation, but a different one for themselves.

It's often the small things that really count!

One more thing about Values: Values must be ordered

So that, in the case of two Values being in conflict, it is clear and easy for all to know which value to stick with, and which must be sacrificed.

E.g.: Disney's top two Values are:

1. Safety
2. Courtesy

If there is a safety issue at a Disney park, then courtesy Values can be sacrificed in order to address the safety issue first. Common sense of course, but then you never know how people sometimes interpret their role!

In fact, if you're finding this Appendix a little hard to digest, then it's worth looking at these successful companies and remembering these Companies are successful because they've paid the price to get their VISION, MISSION and VALUES right, and they've invested significant time and money into making them live., **not the other way round!**

Can you really do this? Of course you can!

Have you ever booked a holiday? If so, this is exactly what you do:

*   VISION: I want a two week break somewhere hot because I've been working hard
*   MISSION: I want to go to Spain in June.
*   VALUES: I want a safe location near the beach

Bingo!

If you want to do some work on this, please start by answering the simple questions on Section Three, Chapter 4 on "Action" and share your work and thoughts with colleagues.

Go on, do it NOW. It won't bite: indeed your colleagues will be very impressed at how deep thinking and proactive you are - give it a try.

I leave you with two items I found on the Internet when researching this material.

1. Here's a lovely simple and clear reference from www.skool.ie

    Direction: It is essential that management sets the targets for the firm and that these are communicated clearly to all the stakeholders. In order to achieve this aim most modern firms adopt a Mission statement. For example the ESB states, "ESB will be a world class company focusing primarily on the energy market, delivering quality products and services to our customers." In addition the managers must establish a corporate culture which encourages the employees to believe in the Mission. In a Sunday Times survey, a company called Capital One was judged to be the third best company to work for in the UK. Its policies included "share options for everyone, casual dress everyday, above average pay, fitness centres, five-week holidays and community involvement."

2. Remember that most dangers come from within. Most brand damage does not arise from product flaws or distribution problems. A lot of it comes from employees or managers who fail to live up to their role as ambassadors of the brand. www.brandfailures.blogspot.com

APPENDIX TWO: Personal organisation (often erroneously called 'Time Management')

Whenever I teach this material, I always make a point of pointing out that:

- it's fine to understand and want to deliver customer service excellence
- **but if you and your colleagues are not well organised personally, you will simply be unable to**

A customer isn't interested that you meant to phone them back, but:

- didn't 'have time'
- were 'just about to do it'
- got 'sidetracked'
- etc, etc.

to them it's simply bad service.

In fact, all these excuses are the same: what they mean is:

- Either, I don't value you as a customer, or
- I don't have a good enough system to enable me to fulfil my promises

So a good (in fact, great) system is VITAL. And, of course, all great things are simple common sense (but so often not common practice).

I am not going to go into detail on time effectiveness (not 'time management' - you can't 'manage time') and there is plenty of material on this vital subject. I will here give a few pointers and helpful tips, but I urge you to study and get to grips with this subject. In a nutshell, however, in order to be effective in this area, you have to do six things (in this order):

1. Accept that it's 'up to you'. No one else controls your time, you do. Be the conductor, not the orchestra.

2. Take time to make sure you know what really matters to you. This will be different for everyone (and will cover the same ground as you will have covered in the 'Mission' work above). As Dr Covey puts it: there's no point making progress hacking through the jungle if it's the wrong jungle!

3. Filter everything on 'importance' not 'urgency'

4. Take the time and effort to set up a good planning system. This is the tool that makes it all work.

5. Execute the plan ruthlessly! It's YOUR life!
    Constantly review, encourage feedback, and strive to improve (we all get it wrong from time to time, but if we're not going forwards, we're going backwards).

6. Let's look at a bit more detail on all of these in turn:

1. Accept that it's 'up to you'.

This is the KEY step. We've covered a lot of this ground already, but until you accept that:

- you control your time
- you control your life
- you CAN say 'no'
- and you don't 'have to' do anything

your ability to use your time effectively will be limited.

Remember:

- There's always too much to do.
- Everyone's 'busy' (at least I've never met anyone who isn't).
- Work expands to fit the time available.
- Things that matter most should never be at the mercy of things that matter least.

And, above all

**how you manage your time is simply a habit
and
habits can be changed**

It may be difficult, it may be uncomfortable and it may very well be un-cool and definitely unglamorous, but effective use of time so often is all of these things.

Just ask most teenagers!

To change your bad habits and turn your vicious circle of wasted time into a virtuous circle of effective use of time effectiveness is simple to understand, but very hard to do, because it takes:

The pain of discipline

The only other option is

The pain of regret

If we aren't self disciplined, then we'll miss opportunities and waste time, which will result in us having some deep regrets.

So it's obvious, we'd all want to be self-disciplined, wouldn't we?

Unfortunately not, because the pain of discipline comes up front, and the pain of regret, comes later. Human motivation is simply

- Towards pleasure, and
- Away from pain

Out of the two, the 'away from pain' is the stronger motivator (products are easier to promote when they remove pain, e.g. anti-wrinkle cream, than if they promote pleasure, e.g. going on holiday). In this scenario, because the pain of discipline comes up front, we tend to try and avoid it (it's often called 'procrastination') and we deal with the pain of regret when it arrives. The pain of regret seems less of a problem, because:

- we don't instigate it, it comes at us
- as it comes at us, we 'have to' deal with it

and so we make up lame excuses like

- 'I haven't got time'
- 'I'm too busy'

And we get stuck in the victim mentality.

If, on the other hand, we take control of our emotions, we accept 'it's up to us' and we change our habits to take the pain of discipline because we know that, in the long run, it'll have the best results (and, by the way, it'll avoid the pain of regret)!

In a nutshell:

Success: is a 'few small disciplines of effectiveness repeated over time'
and
Failure: is a 'few small lapses of discipline repeated over time'

The difference is small and it's that simple, but over time this difference becomes enormous. In the same way, a transatlantic flight will have a significantly different destination with just 1 degree of deviation on the route.

When we really accept it's up to us, we can move to the second step.

2.   **Take time to make sure you know what really matters to you.**

For this step please review the Appendix and main text on 'Mission' and 'Vision'.

Get this right and

You'll know what's 'important' to you.

Get it wrong, or (as in 95% of cases) spend no time thinking about this at all: then you'll have no idea what's important, or where you're trying to get to, so you'll be at the mercy of whatever comes your way, or what other people want you to do. Very stressful and completely unfulfilling.

It's like setting out to sea in a yacht with no idea of which port you're going to, no map and no compass and just 'hoping for the best'. Occasionally it'll be OK, but, usually you'll end up on the rocks.

3.   **Filter everything on 'importance' not 'urgency'.**

This is where most traditional 'time management' material kicks in. The problem is that, if you don't do the above two steps, it's basically impossible to do the third, because you don't know what's IMPORTANT.

So, in effect you can't filter on 'importance', so you make up for this by filtering on 'urgency' and deceive yourself into believing 'urgent' means 'important'. Or you go right back to the beginning and just do what your boss/spouse/parents/children tell you for an 'easy' life. This is the formula for the furthest thing away from an 'easy' life - you know it is!

The best tool to use for filtering is the Time Matrix. Here it is:

	Urgent	**Not Urgent**
Important	**I** ACTIVITIES: Crises Pressing problems Deadline-driven projects	**II** ACTIVITIES: Prevention Relationship building Recreation New opportunities
Not Important	**III** ACTIVITIES: Interruptions Some phone calls Some mail Some meetings Popular activities	**IV** ACTIVITIES: Trivia Some mail Some phone calls Time wasters Pleasure activities

With thanks to FranklinCovey

This is a simple but hugely powerful filtering tool and here's how it works.

The four quadrants represent all the time you have;

- 24 hours a day
- 7 days a week
- 365 days a year

It works by splitting this time into four quadrants, rated by importance and urgency.

Before we look at these quadrants, let's investigate the meaning of the two words 'important' and 'urgent'. Keeping it simple, the words mean this:

- Important: related to my individual or organisational Mission (i.e. it needs to get done in order for me to fulfil my Vision / Mission / and goals). It's stuff that really matters to me.

  - Of course, the real issue here is: different things are 'important' to different people. What is 'important' to me may be trivial to you and more 'importantly', what's 'important' to my boss / spouse / children etc, may also be of no 'importance' to me (though maintaining the relationship may well be 'important'). No wonder people get confused with this. Not only have they never taken the time and paid the price to work out what really is important to them, but also this is different for everyone.

  - And, by the way, we all fundamentally believe that we're 'right', and everyone should agree with us about what's 'important' and what isn't!

- Urgent: simply means it has a timescale that is approaching, **NOTHING ELSE.**

  - The real issue here is that because we've never 'had time' or 'got around to' working out what's 'important' to us, we only have the urgent filter to judge activities by. Most urgent things are not important and important things rarely start off being urgent, but, through our own omission, we are deceived into believing that 'urgent' actually means 'important'.

And this results in stress, aggravation and chaos.

The Quadrants:

Quadrant 1: is the quadrant that holds all the things in your time that are 'important' and 'urgent'. This is called the quadrant of 'necessity', because you need to do these things to survive.

Quadrant 2: is the quadrant that holds all the things in your time that are 'important' and not 'urgent'. This is called the quadrant of 'effectiveness' because this is where all the things that make you effective in your life are held.

Quadrant 3: is the quadrant that holds all the things in your time that are 'urgent' but not 'important'. This is called the quadrant of 'deception' because you are often deceived into thinking the things in here are 'important' because they're 'urgent'.

Quadrant 4: is the quadrant that holds all the things in your time that are not 'important' and not 'urgent'. This is called the quadrant of waste because every activity in this quadrant really is a waste of time.

Some examples of types of activity that you might find in the matrix are shown on the diagram. For our purposes there are three main points to be made:

1. The middle horizontal line is the important one: activities above this are 'important' and therefore worth doing.

   - ACTION: use this tool to filter every activity - is it important? If so, do it, or plan in the time to do it (depending on its size and urgency). If not, get rid of it through delegation and rejection (saying 'no' politely), but remember, never just ignore anything, it will annoy everyone else and one day will come back to bite you.

2. The middle vertical line shows you where these activities will come from.

   - ACTION: Things left of the line (Q1 and Q3) come at you: use the filter, as shown above to know whether this needs actioning (Q1), or whether it's just some trivia, trying to deceive you into believing in its non-existent importance (Q3). When someone says 'It's urgent!' simply reply 'Oh, that's interesting, is it also important?'

   - ACTION: Things right of the line come from you: have the integrity, and pay the price (the pain of discipline) to plan and do the important things at the right time, and to avoid the waste. Know where to draw the line, because important things in Q2, can easily become waste if done to excess. Be self disciplined.

3. The Time Matrix is an excellent tool to use.

   - Remember it.
   - Use it
   - Never surrender to the trivially urgent, that will steal your day and drive you crazy!
   - Take the pain of discipline. Yes, it will seem hard at first, but, after a while it will become a habit, and great one at that!

But, I hear you cry, I don't always 'have time' for the things in Q2, because I spend so much time in Q1!

My challenge is:

- How many things are really in Q1?
- Have you paid the price to know?
- My guess is a LOT of it is actually Q3.
- Are you brave enough to deal with Q3?
- Is your neglect of Q2 resulting in it all moving into Q1?
- Are you so exhausted with Q1 and Q3, you're spending your other time in Q4?

Because the only way you can get more time in Q2, is to get it from Q3 and Q4.   You have to be:

- Courageous and considerate to avoid Q3.
- Clear and ruthless to resist Q4.

4.   Set up a good planning system.

This would take a whole book in itself to explain properly.

Take the pain of discipline to look into it. Go on a course and then get a GREAT (not just a good system). Buy the best. This is the key to success. If you want a recommendation, I'd unreservedly recommend a Franklin Planner from FranklinCovey.

When you've got one:

i.   Plan weekly
- Do this in a quiet place for about 15 minutes BEFORE the week starts.
- Work out what Q2 activities you'd like to achieve during the week (they won't find you, you have to find them).
- Then MAKE APPOINTMENTS in your system for them to happen.
- Then they will.

ii.   Plan daily
- In a quiet place for five minutes
- Review your appointments
- Make a list of the other things
- Review your other 'plannable time'
- Prioritise (Q1, Q2, and a tiny bit of Q3)
- Rank (what order will you do each priority task)
- Estimate time (remember: things usually take much longer than you expect)
- Remember 'life' (things will 'happen' during the day, you need to ensure that you allow time for the unexpected!) and plan some time in for this
- Then schedule them in
  - Compare time of tasks to time available
  - Remember 'life'
  - If there is too much: reassess
  - Cut out / question / delegate
  - Does it have to be done at all?
  - Does it have to be done by me?

Remember, if you don't value and schedule your own time, someone else will.

What will stop you doing all this?

Simply your own self discipline. The pain of discipline is your faithful ally against the thief of time, but he will only be there for you if you embrace him (wholeheartedly).

5.   **Execute the plan ruthlessly!**

It's YOUR life!

Some tips:

- Do the most important tasks in your prime time and lesser ones at other times
- Assess balance of controllable vs. uncontrollable time in your role
- Focus on what you can plan
- Plan time to do the stuff you can't plan as well as you can!
- Book 'catch up' time at the end of the day
- Revisit the plan through the day, be flexible (within the boundaries)
- With project management
- Plan in key actions and milestones
- Block out time for project work
- Be ruthless with your own priorities for you (i.e. Fitness, Continuous Personal Development, Faith and Friends): this affects EVERYTHING else, and is all too easy to let slip in the pressure of everything else

6.   **Constantly review and strive to improve.**

- Analyse time over a week
  - Consider how to spend time more effectively in the future
- Set a timeframe for work each day
  - Work expands to fit the time available
- Analyse in retrospect what was done vs. what is important to success in this role
  - It's easy to be wise in retrospect
  - Different roles have different and often conflicting success criteria
  - Remember the 80 / 20 rule: 80% of the results come from 20% of the actions … focus on the 20% of actions that produce the results you want.
- Make a time log of interruptions / problems
  - Identify the cause: is it your boss, is it someone else, is it the system, or is it in fact yourself?
  - Act: address the cause of the problem, and work with them to resolve it, using the facts you have collected through your time log
- Aim for small changes with continuous improvement
  - Rome wasn't built in a day
- Set SMART goals
  - S = Specific
  - M = Measurable
  - A = Achievable
  - R = Rational
  - T = Time-bound

Remember change means something has to give: are you prepared to pay the price?

And lastly, here are some tips to help you further.

- **We cannot control other people's actions, only OUR REACTION to them.**

- **There will always be more to do than we can possibly cope with.**

- **Work expands to fit the time available.**

- **Failing to plan is planning to fail.**

- **If we don't value our time, others will see us as a cheap resource.**

- **We are responsible for constant review and avoiding bad habits.**

- **Think more, do less.**

Good luck!

Remember: the pain of discipline comes first!

APPENDIX THREE: A Win/Win Agreement

(With thanks to www.franklincovey.com)

Use the 'CFM: Win/Win Agreement Form' overleaf for:

- Goal setting
- Ongoing performance management
- Performance evaluation
- Project planning
- Meeting planning
- Delegation
- Conflict resolution

Its great power lies in it's simplicity and focus upon what 'really matters' - the 'DESIRED RESULTS'.

CFM:	
Win/Win Agreement	
Between	**and**
Subject	
Desired Results (Linked to the CFM)	
Guidelines	
Resources	
Accountability	
Consequences	

APPENDIX FOUR: The Monkey Story (How 'Company Policy' kills Customer Service and Empowerment)

This is a story that is not of my own invention and often does the rounds. I use it here as a great illustration of how simply this can all go wrong and to be used as a 'wake up call' to all those who've read this and said: *"That looks great, but you don't know the problems we have in this organisation, and it just wouldn't apply here."*

Read on, doubting Thomas!

There was once a cage containing five monkeys. Inside the cage, there hung a banana on a string with a set of stairs under it.

Before long, a monkey went to the stairs and started to climb towards the banana. As soon as he touched the stairs, all of the monkeys were sprayed with cold water.

After a while, another monkey made an attempt with the same result - all the monkeys were sprayed with cold water. Pretty soon, when another monkey tried to climb the stairs, the other monkeys prevented it.

Then, the cold water was turned off.

One monkey was removed from the cage and replaced with a new one. The new monkey saw the banana and wanted to climb the stairs. To his surprise and horror, all of the other monkeys attacked him.

After another attempt and attack, he knew that if he tried to climb the stairs, he would be assaulted.

Next, another of the original five monkeys were removed and replaced with a new one. The newcomer went to the stairs and was attacked.

The previous newcomer took part in the punishment with enthusiasm.

Again, a third original monkey was replaced with a new one. The new one made it to the stairs and was attacked as well.

Two of the four monkeys that beat him had no idea why they were not permitted to climb the stairs, or why they were participating in the beating of the newest monkey.

After replacing the fourth and fifth original monkeys, all the monkeys that were sprayed with cold water were replaced. Nevertheless, no monkey ever again approached the stairs.

Why not?

Because as far as they know that's the way it's always been around here.

And that's how company policy begins.

And poor service is just part of the mix - hence, an all too prevailing attitude that "it's more than my job's worth to do anything different to try and resolve it!"

APPENDIX FIVE: Customer focused websites - Hints and Tips

Before I launch into this Appendix, I feel it is important to point out that I am not a web designer or web commerce expert. I have researched this area in order to give some solid common sense tips on customer service excellence in website design and execution.

I would always advise you to use experts in any field of endeavour and websites are no exception, but you need to be aware that website designers are website designers and are not customer service experts in general.

These hints and tips should be used to help you think through your website before you even talk to a website designer and should enable you to present them with a Customer Focused plan of what job you want your website to do.

Not surprisingly, these are ideas that can be arranged in the same format as the main body of this book, so, without further ADO, here are the tips:

1. Remember the audience's needs.

2. Be clear on your Customer Focused Mission: why is the website there and what is it designed to deliver to the customer?

3. What actually matters to the customer (rather than to you)?

4. Go the extra inch.

5. Measure.

In turn:

1. Remember the audience's needs.

- There are billions and billions of websites in the world.
- 99% make no money.
- The average website visitor spends eight to ten seconds on a website.
- Everyone is too busy and no one has enough time.

So, to make your website worthwhile (from everyone's point of view), it needs to be:

- Clear
- Simple
- Focused on your customers' real needs
- VERY easy to use
- Containing real value
- Easy to measure

In web designers' terms, it needs to be 'sticky'.

How do you make it sticky? Well in the same way that you make 'normal' customers come back to you and recommend you to their friends.

2. **Be clear on your Customer Focused Mission: why is the website there and what is it designed to deliver to the customer?**

The first thing to consider is that you won't successfully sell things that you don't believe in. In the same way as mentioned throughout this book, unless you are passionate about your product or service, you will never deliver it excellently, and you will never make good money out of it. So if you aren't passionate about your product or service, find something you are passionate about before you spend out your money on an all singing, all dancing website.

When you've done this you need to be very clear on what your website is designed to deliver to the customer. The customer isn't interested in:

- Your logo
- Your history
- Your pets
- Anything else inane that's important to you

They just have a need, and they want it fulfilled.

In the main, the customer needs the following:

- A clear reason to visit your site (i.e. you'll fulfill their needs quickly, effectively and in a trustworthy manner).
- A clear product explanation they can quickly tell if you're going to be able to fulfil their needs or if they should quickly look elsewhere.
- Useful free content.
- A clear message that you will be able to help them, are trustworthy and will make their life easier. (This can be achieved by having a Customer Focused Mission, aligning all strategy and systems around this and by offering guarantees on price, service, delight etc).
- A clear message that if you can't help them you will say so, or you will point them in the right direction for a better or more cost effective solution.

Don't be tempted to try and make your website all singing and all dancing. The only gizmos and widgets you should consider are those that make the customer's life easier or build trust with you (simple isn't it?).

The customer has very simple needs and if you try and pretend that you are bigger or better connected than you actually are by having a very flash website, it won't take the customer very long to see through this and you will be seen as untrustworthy. If you're a small business, be honest and tell people why this makes you good and easy to deal with.

Be very clear on your short and long-term goals for your site. If you're not clear what you're trying to achieve with your website, your customer certainly won't be. If you don't begin with the end in mind, the customer can easily get confused and misled and this can jeopardise future sales and future service.

Don't try and be too clever, or too crafty: many websites offer some free content, but then make you sign in and give away all your personal details in order to get material and help that's of real value. People are wary to this and it destroys trust.

If you offer real value (and let's face it, the Internet was built on free services), you'll build trust and when the customer wants some real help they'll turn to you first.

3. **What actually matters to the customer (rather than to you)?**

When a customer looks at the website, it's usually because they have a problem that they wish to solve. It's like having a headache, and looking for an aspirin.

You want it quick and you want it easy.

If you want to sell more aspirin than anyone else, you need to do the following:

a. Work out what actually matters to the customer. Marketing rewards reality, not ego. Amazon will tell you where you can buy products cheaper than they can supply them, because they know what actually matters to you as the customer and they are prepared to lose a bit of margin in order to build that trust so that you use them every time. This is such a simple message, but many people miss it.

b. Keep your text simple.

c. Avoid flashiness and fancy stuff unless it adds real value from the customer's point of view.
   The customer just wants to get their aspirin quickly and easily.

d. Avoid adverts: (unless you are very honest about them) they just annoy the customer.

e. Consider your 'landing page': this is the page that the customers first arrive at and is the key page that has to build the message as stated above.

f. Make navigation easy : this can be done by:
   Using simple words
   Popup text explanations
   Speed

g. Anticipate the customer's needs with a simple question and answer section, an easy to use search facility, and a clear sitemap.

h. Build trust by:
   Offering a free and high value newsletter
   Describing recent projects
   Outlining testimonials, good and bad
   Offering genuine free samples
   Charging a fair price for a fair service

i. Have a 'what's new' section if appropriate.

j. Make buying easy and safe by:
   Making it convenient
   Only holding data that you need to fulfil the order, only asking for it once, and making it easy to update.
   Confirming the order when it's been placed. This needs to include details such as list of purchases, address to be delivered, total cost including delivery, date of delivery, and a link to help the customer track the order.
   Offering suggestions of other related purchases, to make life easier for the customer.

k. Be easy to contact. Nothing annoys a customer more than not being able to get the answers to their questions quickly and easily. The Internet and related technology is fantastic for delivering cost effective products and services, but nothing beats the sound of a real voice and the shake of a real hand.

4. Go the extra inch

Websites are getting good at this, but they are still falling down on the Customer Focused Mission. Too many give free and helpful content, but only in return for contact details so that they can then add you to their mailing list.

My advice is give as much away for free as you can and build trust through helpful and positive information, because people generally just want a solution to a problem. Sometimes you will get no business from this, but often the customer may have all the information at their fingertips for free and will still need to employ an expert (that's you) to actually make it work inside their organisation.

Some ways you can do this are:

- Giving free information (simple, short and clear - we've all got too much on our plates already)
- Providing helpful tips in regular newsletters
- Only asking for customers details if there's value in it for the customer
- Keeping it up to date (vital, or you look a wally)
- Offering free audio and video clips
- Offering free online tools (e.g. questionnaires, surveys, tests, calculators)
- Offering an online community (e.g. message boards, blogs or e-mail lists)

In a nutshell, keep looking at the website from the customer's point of view, and make it as simple and easy to use as you possibly can whilst at the same time delivering great value and building trust and loyalty.

5. Measure

As usual, what gets measured gets done.

Measuring 'hits' is very popular, but it often stands for 'how idiots track success': lots of hits and low sales just means that you're wasting lots of people's time. It's much more sensible to measure sales per hit, and time people spend on your site. The better these numbers are, the better you're doing the job above.

And, of course, do include on your website the ability for people to feedback on your service and systems easily and do ensure you contact them and thank them for doing so.

TO SUM UP

The Internet is a desert: the only really successful websites, in the long run, are those that deliver the true Customer Focused Mission. These are the oases in the desert.

In fact, the Internet is the tool that is and will empower the customer greater than anything that has gone before.

The Internet is currently starved of two things:

- Proper, helpful information
- Real content

Give these, in a Customer Focused way, and you'll be on the right track.

APPENDIX SIX: Why 'Customer Satisfaction Surveys' Don't Work

The customer is king. Those who please the customer best win. When being surveyed, **customers just want to tell you their views, not answer your questions**. Winners are fanatical about enabling them to do this as easily as possible.

Here are the eleven key reasons why traditional customer satisfaction surveys don't work.

1. They're too long. The customer just wants to be listened to. They don't want to have to fill in loads of data.

2. Their questions are not Customer Focused. They're written by the Company. Come on - the customer just wants to feed back to you as easily as possible. T hey don't want to answer your questions!\

3. They're marketing in disguise. The customer sees you want their phone number, email and inside leg measurement - they aren't fooled. They have enough 'spam' to deal with already and anyway, they don't want to tell you their age and what car they drive, they just want to tell you about your service.

4. They often actually detract from the customer service. Because the customer just wants to be 'listened' to and they don't do this!

5. They have low response rates. Because of the above, response rates are usually very low (this is a huge issue). So the only people who end up telling you what they think are either those with a grudge, or those with time on their hands. Hardly likely to produce valuable information.

6. They produce no clear 'action points'. Because there are too many questions and not enough answers, often the data can be challenged, even if it did make sense. If it's good data, there's usually too little to break down meaningfully across Divisions or Departments.

7. They're out of date before they're published. These surveys are often an 'event', then the results are analysed (because they're too complicated), so by the time the average Joe sees them, they're a couple of months out of date and no use at all.

8. They actually make the situation worse. Because of the above, what actually happens is that the wrong customers influence the decisions, the good customers don't bother and the employees just get fed up.

9. They don't identify the real issues. It's a lottery!

10. They produce no clear 'score', so they have no real value.

11. We don't want 'satisfied' customers; we want 'delighted' ones!

APPENDIX SEVEN: Customer Service Quotes

I hope you find some inspiration and fun in these.

"Accept the fact that we have to treat almost anybody as a volunteer." - Peter Drucker

"Efficiency is doing things right; effectiveness is doing the right things." - Peter Drucker

"Follow effective action with quiet reflection. From the quiet reflection will come even more effective action.." - Peter Drucker

"Knowledge has to be improved, challenged, and increased constantly, or it vanishes." - Peter Drucker

"No institution can possibly survive if it needs geniuses or supermen to manage it. It must be organised in such a way as to be able to get along under a leadership composed of average human beings." - Peter Drucker

"Suppliers and especially manufacturers have market power because they have information about a product or a service that the customer does not and cannot have, and does not need if he can trust the brand. This explains the profitability of brands." - Peter Drucker

"The aim of marketing is to know and understand the customer so well the product or service fits him and sells itself." - Peter Drucker

"The only thing we know about the future is that it will be different." - Peter Drucker

"Today knowledge has power. It controls access to opportunity and advancement." - Peter Drucker

"A man is what he thinks about all day long." - Ralph Waldo Emerson

"Always do what you are afraid to do." - Ralph Waldo Emerson

"Common sense is genius dressed in its working clothes." - Ralph Waldo Emerson

"Doing well is the result of doing good. That's what capitalism is all about." - Ralph Waldo Emerson

"Shallow men believe in luck. Strong men believe in cause and effect." - Ralph Waldo Emerson

"The fox has many tricks. The hedgehog has but one. But that is the best of all." - Ralph Waldo Emerson

"A good head and a good heart are always a formidable combination." - Nelson Mandela

"If you talk to a man in a language he understands, that goes to his head. If you talk to him in his language, that goes to his heart." - Nelson Mandela

"There is no passion to be found playing small - in settling for a life that is less than the one you are capable of living." - Nelson Mandela

"Feedback is the breakfast of champions." - Ken Blanchard

"The productivity of a work group seems to depend on how the group members see their own goals in relation to the goals of the organisation." - Ken Blanchard

"There are three constants in life. Change, choice and principles." - Stephen Covey

"In this life we cannot do great things. We can only do small things with great love." - Mother Teresa

"Spread love everywhere you go. Let no one ever come to you without leaving happier." - Mother Teresa

"The biggest disease today is not leprosy or tuberculosis, but rather the feeling of being unwanted." - Mother Teresa

"We ourselves feel that what we are doing is just a drop in the ocean. But the ocean would be less because of that missing drop." - Mother Teresa

"No one is useless in this world who lightens the burdens of another." - Charles Dickens

"There is no higher religion than human service: to work for the common good is the greatest creed " - Albert Schweitzer

"If you aren't going all the way, why go at all?" - Joe Namath

"All for one and one for all ." - Alexandre Dumas

"We must all hang together, or, most assuredly, we shall all hang separately." - Benjamin Franklin

"Beware the barrenness of a busy life." - Socrates

"Employ your time in improving yourself by other men's writings, so that you shall gain easily what others have laboured hard for." - Socrates

"I am the wisest man alive, for I know one thing, and that is that I know nothing." - Socrates

"Let him that would move the world first move himself." - Socrates

"Be the change you want to see in the world." - Gandhi

"Service which is rendered without joy helps neither the servant nor the served. But all other pleasures and possessions pale into nothingness before service which is rendered in a spirit of joy." - Gandhi

"That service is the noblest which is rendered for its own sake." - Gandhi

"All things appear and disappear because of the concurrence of causes and conditions. Nothing ever exists entirely alone; everything is in relation to everything else." - Buddha

"Believe nothing, no matter where you read it, or who said it, no matter if I have said it, unless it agrees with your own reason and your own common sense." - Buddha

"I do not believe in a fate that falls on men however they act; but I do believe in a fate that falls on them unless they act." - Buddha

"The only real failure in life is not to be true to the best one knows." - Buddha
What is the appropriate behaviour for a man or a woman in the midst of this world, where each person is clinging to his piece of debris? What's the proper salutation between people as they pass each other in this flood?" - Buddha

"The superior man understands what is right; the inferior man understands what will sell." - Confucius

"The will to win, the desire to succeed, the urge to reach your full potential, these are the keys that will unlock the door to personal excellence." - Confucius

"You cannot open a book without learning something." - Confucius

"I hate quotations. Tell me what you know." - Ralph Waldo Emerson

APPENDIX EIGHT: Customer Service SWOT

I am the greatest strength in your organisation
… but I am often overlooked and ignored
I think you're OK and I want to be your trusted friend, and a source of strength and growth
I can ensure your business thrives for years and years
Or I can drain you of energy and resources
All you need to do is to listen to me and change with my needs
… but you won't
… so I can't help you as I want to
I am your customer
If you don't look after me, someone else will

I am the greatest weakness in your organisation
I am usually only 'satisfied' by you, and I am looking for something better
So when someone a little bit better comes along, I'll leave you
I don't want to do this
But you aren't truly focused on my needs and desires … and your systems reflect this
… and you won't listen to me
So, as soon as I get a chance … I'll go
And I'll weaken you until you perish
I am your customer
If you don't look after me, someone else will

I am the greatest opportunity in your organisation
I want to help you build a truly great organisation … for nothing!
And I cost very little to keep
In order to allow me to do this, you need to really value me and listen to me
But you don't seem to want to
So I can't help you nearly as much as I want to, and eventually I'll get fed up and stop trying
And you'll suffer from lack of ideas, and eventually you'll be unable to meet my needs for the
future
So I'll go
I am your customer
If you don't look after me, someone else will

I am the greatest threat to your organisation
If I think you're 'great', I'll tell a couple of my closest friends,
If you make a mistake, I won't tell you … but I will tell everyone else
If I'm 'satisfied', I'll stay with you only until someone else grabs my attention
(which is not very long)
My deepest desire is to be your friend and partner
I want to trust you and make both our lives easier
… but you won't listen to me
I can ruin your business overnight: history shows countless times when I've done this
I am your customer
If you don't look after me, someone else will.

APPENDIX NINE: ACTION PLAN

If you haven't done it yet, do not pass 'GO', do not close this book, do not collect £200.

Go back to Section Three, Chapter 4 on "Action" and do it!

… and keep a sharp eye out for problems, because they will surely come, whether you're prepared or not.

Remember:

"There are only two mistakes one can make along the road to truth; not going all the way, and not starting." - Buddha

"You may delay, but time will not." - Benjamin Franklin.

Bibliography

If you want to continue to develop and excel, I can highly recommend these as excellent resources.

Book	Author	Reference
The 7 Habits of Highly Effective People	Dr. Steven R. Covey	Simon & Schuster Ltd
Why men don't listen and women can't read maps	Alan & Barbara Pease	Orion Publishing
The Speed of Trust	Steven M. R. Covey	Simon & Schuster Ltd
Fish!	Stephen C. Lundin, Harry Paul & John Christensen	Mobius
Raving Fans	Ken Blanchard & Sheldon Bowles	Harper Collins
The Ultimate Question	Fred Reicheld	Harvard Business School Press
The Art of Exceptional Living	Jim Rohn	Nightingale Conant
Customer Service for Dummies	Karen Leland & Keith Bailey	John Wiley & Sons
The Dilbert Principle	Scott Adams	Boxtree Ltd
The Art of the Start	Guy Kawasaki	Portfolio
Good to Great	Jim Collins	Random House
Moments of Truth	Jan Carlzon	Harper Collins
Sydney Harbour Bridge Visitor Centre		
The One Minute Manager	Ken Blanchard & Spencer Johnson	Harper Collins
Empowerment Takes More Than a Minute	Ken Blanchard, John Carlos & Alan Randolph	Berrett-Koehler
Let's Get Real or Let's Not Play	Mahan Khalsa	Franklin Covey
The Art of Happiness	The Dalai Lama & Howard Cutler	Mobius
Man's Searching for Meaning	Victor Frankl	Rider & Co
The Heart of Success	Rob Parsons	Hodder & Stoughton

'Great or Poor' Unique Special Offer

I hope you have enjoyed 'Great or Poor' and have found many things that you can take back to your Organisation to improve your results.

As you know, most great ideas are easier to understand than to implement and you may need some help.

Of course, Great or Poor would love to do further business with you, but here's an offer that is more than that. Using the voucher below, I'd like to offer you a 20% discount on your first consultancy or training (or both).

Great or Poor can help you make these principles work in your Organisation through consultancy, training, coaching, mentoring and measuring. And remember, all prices are transparent and services guaranteed.

I look forward to hearing from you.

Guy Arnold

Simply contact us via
http://customer-service.championsclubcommunity.com
quoting "GORP 1/20"
to receive a **20% discount** off your first
Consultancy or Training with us.